The Morning After

Also by Stephen J. Wall and Shannon Rye Wall

The New Strategists: Creating Leaders at All Levels

THE
MORNING
AFTER

Making Corporate Mergers
Work After the Deal Is Sealed

STEPHEN J. WALL AND
SHANNON RYE WALL

PERSEUS PUBLISHING
Cambridge, Massachusetts

Many of the designations used by manufacturers and sellers to distinguish their products are claimed as trademarks. Where those designations appear in this book and Perseus Books was aware of a trademark claim, the designations have been printed in initial capital letters.

A CIP record for this book is available from the Library of Congress.
ISBN 0-7382-0371-8

Perseus Publishing is a member of the Perseus Books Group.

Text design by Heather Hutchison
Set in 11-point Janson by the Perseus Books Group

Perseus Publishing titles are available at special discounts for bulk purchases in the U.S. by corporations, institutions, and other organizations. For more information, please contact the Special Markets Department at HarperCollins Publishers, 10 East 53rd Street, New York, NY 10022, or call 212-207-7528.

Find us on the World Wide Web at
http://www.perseuspublishing.com
http://www.themorningafterbook.com

1 2 3 4 5 6 7 8 9 10–03 02 01 00
First printing, October 2000

For Lance Mitchell, Tom Waltermire, and Don Knechtges
Clients, colleagues, and friends
who are a continuing source of insight and inspiration

CONTENTS

ACKNOWLEDGMENTS

Our sincere appreciation to these people who helped us with this book:

- Our sources: Those of you who gave your advice and time to be interviewed for this book. Your experiences and wisdom have inspired us greatly.
- Our clients: Together, we have learned many of the lessons contained in this book. In particular, we thank all of our colleagues at PolyOne, PaineWebber, and MetLife for many years of productive partnership.
- Our project team: Evelyn Toynton and Jon Briscoe were full members of the project team throughout the process, and each contributed much time, talent, and expertise. We *really* couldn't have done it without you. Thanks also to project team members Marie Boccuzzi and Kelley Joy at Right Manus and to our creative and patient editor, Nick Philipson, and our wonderful agent, Barbara Rifkind.
- Our Right Manus partners, Rick Lepsinger and Toni Lucia, and their partners, Bonnie Usliander and Allyn Keiser: Thank you for so *many* years of fun, work, support, commiseration, and love.
- Our other colleagues at Right Manus: We couldn't imagine a better team. Thanks to Alissa Abbey, Janet Castricum, Kristy Christiano, Jeff Cicone, Howard Cohen, Cécile Derisson, Stan Hubbard, Bill Jockle, Marc Kaplan, Terri Lowe, Tamika Moss, Sid Nachman, Jennifer Owler, Judy Provoost, J. T. Rehill, Susanne Reilly, Michelle Rodriguez, Ian Shearson, Thomas

Spinelli, Kim Tamru, Laurie Tubbs, and Patty Wilson. Thanks also to Chris Pierce-Cooke at Right Management Consultants for your support of this project.

- Our other readers who provided insightful and very helpful comments on the manuscript: Denis Belzile, Sissy Caldwell, Diane Davie, Glenn Goldman, Bob Grimes, Don Knechtges, Steve Krupp, Lance Mitchell, Harold Scharlatt, Carol Ann Taggart, Sandy Wall, Tom Waltermire, and Chris Walton. Very special thanks to Jean Turrentine, Arch Turrentine, and Blair Murray for their detailed comments on the entire draft.
- Our family and friends: Thanks for your love and support. Many, many thanks to Jack Wall and Dave Wall for giving us the time to work on this book, and to Alissa and Marc Berger for giving us Samantha Anne.

PREFACE

If there is a single underlying belief that is guaranteed to doom a merger, it is surely this: *Once the deal is sealed, the hard work is over.* In reality, it is after the deal is announced and the negotiators celebrate that the real work begins—the morning after and for many, many more days to come.

M. Scott Peck began his book *The Road Less Traveled* with this sentence: "Life is difficult."[1] When you can accept that, you can go on from there. Mergers and acquisitions are also difficult. When you recognize that fact, you can start down the road that will lead to success.

Too often, however, people grossly underestimate the difficulty and the amount of time, energy, and resources that are required to integrate two organizations. When mergers are handled poorly, and they often are, value is lost, people's lives are turned upside down, and the company, more often than not, emerges weaker than it was before the deal.

The consequences of neglecting to attend to post-acquisition integration include declining business results; power struggles that waste energy, resources, and brain power; waning morale; anxiety, confusion, and uncertainty; and a mass exodus of key talent.

This turmoil has, research suggests, a very real and very negative effect on the bottom lines of many merged companies. More often than not, mergers and acquisitions destroy shareholder value, even when the strategic rationale for the combination is logically compelling. In many cases, the cause of the failure is that the post-deal integration is neglected or handled poorly.

The toll that poor merger management is taking on companies and the people in them is enormous. Listen to Vice President of Executive and Management Development Grace MacArthur of ARCO, which was acquired in 2000 by BP Amoco after a lengthy regulatory battle:

Fundamentally, mergers and acquisitions are very negative at the end of the day for employees, for their families, and for the communities they live in. We are going to have to take a real look at the human cost of mergers and acquisitions—I think it's significant, and it's negative, for the most part. We've been on an emotional roller coaster. It's unbelievable the stress that people have been through.[2]

As we interviewed people for this book, we were struck by the strength and depth of their emotions and by how profoundly most acquisitions affect everyone involved. This book includes a lot of quotes from folks who have "been there"; their stories are a compelling reminder of very human impact of merger-related decisions.

If the merger mania is not going to stop and, for some compelling reasons, we don't believe it is, there is a critical need to manage the integration process much more deliberately and effectively.

While examples of failed mergers far outnumber examples of successful ones, there *are* some companies that have learned how to integrate acquisitions well. We'll refer to these companies repeatedly: Cisco Systems, Geon (now PolyOne), and Affiliated Computer Services are three of the successful acquirers that are highlighted. We studied their philosophies and merger processes in detail in order to identify best practices; these can serve as useful guidelines to be adopted and adapted by others faced with the task of integrating two companies.

Our own experience with integrating acquisitions goes back fifteen years; part of our practice focuses on helping senior teams formulate and implement strategies successfully. More and more, this work began to involve formulating acquisition strategies and criteria, assessing acquisition candidates and their senior management talent, and developing and implementing plans for the integration of the two entities after the deal is done.

In 1993, when PaineWebber acquired Kidder Peabody, we worked on the entire acquisition process from both sides, from the beginning all the way through the integration. Since then, our firm has worked to help integrate many acquisitions, including Chase–Manufacturers Hanover, Chase–Chemical Bank, Pfizer–Warner-Lambert, and almost ten different acquisitions for Geon. In May 2000, Geon announced its merger with M. A. Hanna to become the largest polymer service and technology company in the world: PolyOne.

Who Should Read This Book?

Our aim is to provide practical, readable, real-world information and advice that builds on the research and summarizes the best thinking in the area of merger integration. This book should be particularly useful if you:

- Are involved in the merger integration process in your company
- Are considering buying or selling a company
- Want to understand how the process works, what you might expect, and how you can survive and thrive during a merger

A Note on the Terms "Merger" and "Acquisition"

For reasons that will be explained later, we don't believe that true "mergers of equals" are possible or advisable. Every union of two companies is an acquisition; as one executive said, "This was supposed to be a merger, but as we know, none of these things is really a merger. There is always a top dog."[3]

Throughout this book, we'll use the term "acquisition" to refer to the deal itself and the terms "merger" and "merging" to refer to the integration process that begins the morning after and continues for many months and even years.

An Overview of *The Morning After*

In this book, our focus is on what happens after the deal is announced. How can leaders manage the integration well? How can they increase the likelihood that the newly merged organization will emerge as a stronger company, providing increased value to its customers?

Still, the quality of the "morning after" depends to a great extent on what happened before. There are a number of factors that need to be attended to and managed early in the deal-making process in order for the integration to be successful, and we've addressed these as well.

TABLE F.1   Guide to Book Contents

Chapter	Read This Chapter If You Want to Know More About
Part 1: The Foundation for Success	
Chapter 1. Acquiring the Future: New Foundations of Competitive Advantage	What's driving the acquisition mania, and why are so many companies joining together?
Chapter 2. Warning Signs: Danger Ahead!	What are the early warning signs that a merger is headed down the wrong road? What are the major pitfalls involved with merging two companies?
Chapter 3. Steering Clear of Disaster: Best Practices of Successful Acquirers	What are successful companies doing to integrate acquisitions effectively?
Chapter 4. The Mating Dance: From Selection of Partner to Announcement of Intent to Merge	Why do leaders choose to acquire other companies or sell their own? What does the deal process involve?
Chapter 5. "What Have I Gotten Myself Into?" Due Diligence and Pre-Close Integration Planning	What happens between the time the deal is announced and when it closes? What can be done during this time to smooth the integration of the two companies?
Part 2: After the Deal Is Sealed	
Chapter 6. Creating the Future Together: Staffing the Senior Team and Clarifying the Strategic Direction	Who should be on the leadership team? How can leaders create a shared strategy and vision of the future for the new organization?
Chapter 7. Form Follows Function: Arriving at the Integration Strategy	Alignment, synthesis, or consolidation? How do you determine the optimal amount of integration necessary for success?
Chapter 8. Making the Marriage Work: Managing the Merger	How are "best-practice" companies managing the actual integration process? Who is involved, and what do they do?
Chapter 9. Who Does What to Whom? Organizational Design and Staffing	How do leaders determine what the new organizational chart will look like and who will fill what roles?
Chapter 10. Getting the Message Out—and Back: Communications During Mergers	What are some best practices related to communicating with employees and other key stakeholders during the integration process?

(continues)

(continued)

An Invitation

As we all continue to learn more about this very young discipline, it's important that we continue to identify innovative approaches and best practices. What are you doing in your company to manage the merger process well? What's working? What's keeping you up at night? We invite you to visit our web site: <http://www.themorningafter book.com> to share your thoughts and learn from others facing the same challenges. We look forward to hearing from you.

Part One

THE FOUNDATION
FOR SUCCESS

1

ACQUIRING
THE FUTURE

New Foundations of
Competitive Advantage

*It takes all the running you can do to keep in the same place. If
you want to get somewhere else, you must run at least twice as
fast as that.*

—Lewis Carroll, *Through the Looking Glass*

Throughout the late 1990s, businesses around the world were seized
by a marriage frenzy. Citicorp-Travelers. Daimler Benz–Chrysler.
GTE–Bell Atlantic. Exxon-Mobil. Viacom-CBS. Vodafone–AirTouch.
Almost every week, another mega-merger was announced, and another record was broken. In 1997, the total value of mergers and acquisitions worldwide reached a record-breaking $1.58 trillion,[1] a
figure that was superseded the next year, when the numbers shot to a
staggering $2.4 trillion.[2] The total for 1999 was $3.44 trillion,[3] and
there's no slowdown in sight.

If anything, the pace is quickening and the stakes are getting higher:
January 2000 brought the announcement of the mammoth America

Online (AOL)–Time Warner merger; the combined market value of these two giants is estimated at $350 billion. In February, we saw the spectacular hostile takeover of Mannesmann by Vodafone AirTouch for $183 billion—the largest such takeover in history.

What's going on here? Why are companies rushing to the altar more than ever before?

Globalization?

Is the desire to join forces being driven by the globalization trend? This can certainly be put forth as a strong argument. As customers become more global, the companies that serve them must do so as well. We're seeing this with the Tier 1 suppliers (manufacturers of automobile components) in the automobile industry, for example; this is finally becoming a truly global industry, with most of the major manufacturers producing "world cars" around the globe. Developing a global presence through cross-border acquisitions is an increasingly common strategy.

For many companies, the pressure to globalize comes not only from their customers but from competitors as well. In order to compete within a given industry, businesses need access to the same markets, a similar cost of capital, and a profile comparable to that of their competitors. If competitors are becoming more global in reach, other businesses in the industry must do so as well just to maintain a level playing field.

Economies of Scale?

Globalization is a strong contributor to the corporate marriage mania, but it is certainly not the only factor. In many industries, intense pressures on profit margins have created an ever-increasing need to achieve greater efficiencies and economies of scale.

Acquisitions are a logical solution, and the achievement of "synergies" is the purported goal. To many people, the word "synergy" has become synonymous with "Plants and offices will be closing soon." Cost savings and economies of scale are only one of a number of synergies that may be gained from an acquisition; however, since they are often the most easily quantifiable, they are also the most frequently predicted and discussed.

In industries that are breathlessly consolidating, such as the global automobile and financial services industries, the mandate is "eat or be eaten." The frenzy is so great, in some cases, that acquisitions essentially represent a survival strategy. In such cases, the decision to merge may not be always subject to a careful strategic analysis that specifies the capabilities that both sides can bring to the combination.

This may be one reason that mergers in rapidly consolidating industries have been markedly unsuccessful. In the pharmaceutical industry, for example, the *Economist* reported in January 2000 that "with one exception, every big drug merger since 1970 has led to a subsequent loss in market share" (see Figure 1.1).[4]

FIGURE 1.1   A Cure Worse Than the Disease

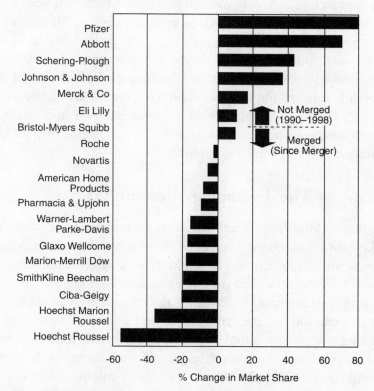

% Change in Market Share

SOURCE: "The New Alchemy," *Economist*, January 22, 2000.

Even with this powerful evidence that merged companies historically lag behind nonmerged competitors in the pharmaceutical industry, Pfizer CEO William Steere shifted his company's strategy radically in 2000 by acquiring Warner-Lambert. His bet is that the rules of the game are changing and that the addition of Warner-Lambert's products and pipeline of new drugs will enhance Pfizer's already strong position.

In some industries, "bigger" is indeed necessary for a company to achieve competitive advantage. Paul Marsh of the London Business School found that while small publicly held businesses in Britain and the United States outperformed large ones overall from the mid-1950s to the end of the 1980s, that trend has now been dramatically reversed.[5] The bigger companies really are doing better, so much so that it has even been suggested that if small public companies actually left the market entirely, it would probably have a beneficial effect on the economy—a novel idea.[6]

Of course, bigger is not *always* better. Economies of scale result from sound strategy, careful management, and attentive allocation of resources, not from size alone. We all know the danger; when companies get big, they too often lose their edge and their ability to be innovative and responsive. Still, at the dawn of the twenty-first century, the conclusion in many cases is that "size matters." The words of the seventeenth-century philosopher Thomas Hobbes are particularly apt now: "He cannot be content with a moderate power ... because he cannot assure the power and means to live well, which he hath [at] present, without the acquisition of more."[7]

The Technology Revolution?

In addition to globalization and the need for economies of scale, another key driver behind the acquisition boom is certainly the explosion of information technology and technology-based systems and services. The high-tech industry itself is a widely publicized hotbed of acquisition activity, making many millionaires and creating a talent drain that more mature businesses are struggling to deal with.

The technology revolution is affecting small and medium-sized companies in many other industries as well. As technology becomes more and more of a vital factor in gaining competitive advantage, smaller organizations may lack the capital they need to keep pace. As business-to-business e-commerce explodes, companies find that they need to spend more on enterprise-wide systems that link them to their customers and help them manage their business more effectively internally. This kind of investment can be out of reach for smaller firms; therefore, they're joining forces with organizations that have deeper pockets as well as experience with emerging technologies.

The Internet era has also contributed to the globalization and commoditization of many products and services. It has provided both corporate and individual consumers with unprecedented global reach and information, requiring suppliers, in turn, to make their offerings available more widely and more inexpensively than ever before. In order to meet these new challenges, companies are joining forces in record numbers, marrying distribution with content à la AOL–Time Warner.

Deregulation?

In a number of industries, the acquisition boom has been propelled by the removal of regulatory handcuffs by governmental and other agencies. The U.S. financial services industry, which had been undergoing massive consolidation and restructuring, had long lobbied for the repeal of the 1933 Glass-Steagall Act, which restricted the degree to which banks, insurance companies, and securities firms could enter one another's territories. In 1999, the repeal of Glass-Steagall added flames to the acquisition bonfire; this time, insurance firms are at the center of the action. Banks are engulfing insurers, and insurers are rushing to acquire or be acquired.

In the United States, the long-anticipated deregulation in the utilities industry is also driving a number of mergers as utilities search for better profits by offering new services "beyond the meter." Buying up infrastructure contractors has become a common diversification strategy in this industry. Utilities are also attempting to get into the hot telecom field (which was itself significantly deregulated in 1996).

These are risky strategies driven by the need for better profitability; the ability of the utilities to actually integrate these diverse acquisitions has yet to be proven. The different cultures of the two industries are likely to present some major merger challenges: As the *New York Times* noted, "It takes time to master the mosh pit after a lifetime of the minuet."[8]

Likewise, in Europe, the merger activity is showing a marked increase as the European Union lowers some of the regulatory barriers between countries. The 1999 introduction of a common currency, along with the rush to globalize and privatize companies, has prompted the beginning of an acquisition boom. Observers say this is quickly reshaping the face of European businesses and of companies around the world that compete with them.

Senior Management Incentives and Egos?

Are the real driving forces behind the acquisitions boom the incentives and egos of CEOs and other senior leaders, as some in the business press have suggested? Think back to the 1980s, when the leaders of companies fought ferociously against being acquired. This has changed only in the last decade, with the advent of senior-management stock options—the value of which can soar with an acquisition.

Many top executives' incentive packages are now structured to make it hugely profitable for them to accept a takeover. That's what happened at Chrysler, where Robert Eaton cashed out $70 million in Chrysler options and received new options in DaimlerChrysler.[9] (He resigned in early 2000, saying that his goals had been achieved.) The top three executives at Bankers Trust Company got $122 million over three years when the company, which had lost $6 million the previous year, was acquired by Deutsche Bank in 1999.[10]

Sweetening the deal for top executives in an acquired company is a trend that is spreading to Europe, as well. Mannesmann's reluctant-to-be-overtaken CEO, Klaus Esser, was awarded an "appreciation award" of 31.8 million marks ($16.04 million) in early 2000. Shortly after the deal, an analyst quoted in the *Wall Street Journal* predicted that the proliferation of golden parachutes for European senior executives will "spark long-term changes just as they did in the U.S. a decade ago."[11]

Ego might well be a factor as well. What better way for a CEO to leave a legacy than to make the big acquisition that is splashed on the cover of *Business Week*?

The point here is that mergers are driven by strong human, emotional, and personal factors, in addition to sweeping global, economic, and industry trends. The decision to merge and acquire is made by individuals, and their decisions have visceral, real ramifications for many, many more people down the road. The desire to win, the need for recognition and validation, the positive push to "do something big" are key drivers of the acquisition acceleration that is affecting so many people's business lives.

The New Super Equation

All of these factors—globalization, the resurgence of advantages based on size, the technology revolution, deregulation, and the very real personal motives of leaders—have played a part in various acquisitions over the past decade, with more than one applying in most cases. These catalysts, along with several others, are prompting a sweeping evolutionary trend, or "Super Equation," that is transforming business as we know it.

The Super Equation has three main components: Superheated competition, supersmart customers, and superfast change.

Competition is hotter. To survive in the marketplace, the whole organization needs to be focused on increasing the value perceived by the customer; this requirement to differentiate the organization from the competition has become urgent on a daily as well as longer-term basis.

A complacent business is a soon-to-be-dead business. This is old news to the once all-powerful American auto companies. Likewise, many utility companies that failed to anticipate the effects of deregulation have been swallowed up by the competitors who took the initiative to reshape themselves in the early 1980s through the early 1990s, when the handwriting was on the wall.

Customers are smarter. They are so smart about what they need, they tell us before we can figure it out. They articulate what they need us to be that we're currently not; if we can't fulfill those needs now, they will go elsewhere—now. As we'll discuss in more detail later in this chapter, Cisco Systems uses input from customers to drive its business strategy.

Armed with real-time information, customers are much more knowledgeable and demanding than they ever were. Car buyers, for example, can walk into a dealership with a printout of what the dealer paid for a car. This means that customers' loyalty has to be continuously earned. Leaders need to ensure that they have continuous customer feedback that is used to catalyze change in the organization.

Change is faster.   For most of us, the ability to keep up on a day-to-day basis with changes that are occurring exceeds our ability to scan the environment and certainly to incorporate those changes into our ways of working and living. As difficult as this is for us as individuals, it may be even harder for business organizations to keep pace with the changes that are occurring.

In this superchanging environment, the mandate for every business is *evolve to survive*. Charles Darwin said, "It's not the strongest species that survive, nor the most intelligent, but the ones most responsive to change."[12]

The world in which corporations compete is one in which constant flux has become the norm. Change cannot follow our once-orderly models of "plan, implement, and then sustain." People who studied organizations in the 1960s and 1970s were trained in a three-step model posited by Kurt Lewin. In the first step, the work was to "unfreeze" the organization from its current state. Then, theoretically at least, we moved through the "transition" phase, where the real change occurred. Finally, we got to the "refreeze" stage, where the change was solidified. Tough work, but if leaders could move people in the organization through it, everyone could get back to the "real work."

Now, change *is* the real work. Lewin's model looks, with perfect hindsight, like an incredible luxury. Instead of the unfreeze-transition-refreeze sequence, the best we have is continual slush. Constant churn. Constant flux. Some among us find this invigorating and refreshing. Others long for slower, more predictable times.

Succeeding in a Slushy World

In a slushy world in constant flux, leaders are finding that their companies' strategies need to shift fairly frequently in order for their businesses to survive. There is, as there always was, a need for long-term vision, deliberate plans, and accountability for reaching established goals. More than ever, however, there is a countervailing need for allowing strategies to evolve in response to changing customer needs and marketplace realities.[13]

Every new evolving strategy, market, and configuration of assets brings with it the need for a different set of skills, experience, and organizational capabilities. Increasingly, it is becoming impossible to develop all those skills and capabilities in-house. Given the dramatic pace of change, there is simply not enough time to undergo the long developmental process required, at least not if a company hopes to respond to market changes as they occur. A manufacturer of disk drives can't become a purveyor of complex software solutions merely by deciding it wants to be. A pharmaceutical company can't launch a bioengineering research initiative overnight. That's one reason acquisitions have become so important and so ubiquitous.

Listen to Phil Garner, former Senior Director of Engineering for the high-tech acquirer 3Com and now Vice President, Engineering, for Emware, Inc.: "The rate of change has become so high in our industry that it is just about impossible to plan your internal developments in such a way that you will have the right technology at the right time. You really have to think about going outside to some little company that might have, through luck or insight, developed the right technology."[14]

AT&T's recognition that it could not possibly develop all the technology it would need to offer its customers "one-stop shopping" led it to a 1999 $60-billion deal to buy TCI Communications, the second-largest cable company in the United States. In addition, in 2000, AT&T acquired cable giant MediaOne Group, which also owns a 25.5 percent share of Time Warner Entertainment (TWE).

The deal was approved by the Federal Communications Commission (FCC) with the stipulation that the new entity divest some of its holdings. Even with the divestiture, AT&T will have made huge inroads into the fast-growing Internet and cable television markets.[15]

The Protean Organization

All of this leads us to suggest a model of effective organizations based on experience and what works in the new real world. We call it the "protean organization," after the Greek god Proteus. When a mortal was chasing him, Proteus could transform himself instantly into a tree or a pillar of fire or a boar; in that way, he eluded his pursuers. Like Proteus, modern business organizations need the ability to change shape at will in the face of competitive threats and in the pursuit of opportunities.

Becoming a protean business is the ultimate "stretch" goal, and not one that is ever ultimately accomplished. It involves continuous striving toward a state of readiness, agility, and organizational vigilance. The companies referred to as protean in this book are not perfect; however, their leaders recognize the reality of constant change and the need for continuous adaptation. Adding new competencies through acquisition is a core strategy in the battle to succeed in whatever world emerges—and in many cases, these successful protean companies become shapers of that world.

Leaders of protean organizations recognize the need for:

1. An approach to strategy that is both deliberate and evolutionary. They realize that strategy should be both planned and allowed to emerge in response to new information and developments in the industry.
2. An organizational structure that is networked, fluid, organic, and process driven. They emphasize flexibility in the way they design work and in reporting relationships.
3. A constant reassessment of their capabilities related to the changing demands of the marketplace. They continuously add to the company's skill base and intellectual assets; they also get rid of those components that no longer fit their mission and strategy.

Going beyond this intellectual recognition, protean organizations have developed the core competencies needed to transform themselves repeatedly as market opportunities arise. Growth is dependent on expanding their intellectual resources so that the talent will be there to respond to market shifts and deal with new situations as they arise. When leaders of these companies make acquisitions, they are often "purchasing" people, with all their knowledge, expertise, and skills. With this comes the need to manage the human, emotional aspects of the acquisition with even greater care and attention.

Acquisitions can be a powerful and logical way for an organization to capture the resources it needs to remain flexible and competitive. At its best, the integration process itself becomes an opportunity to develop the skills the organization will need to achieve advantage. An integration is the ultimate "work-out"—a chance to eliminate work or transactions from a company's business processes. It can be the catalyst for refining those processes so that they work better than ever. A company that can execute an integration successfully, in all its complexity, will be able to do a lot of other things successfully, too.

Success Story: Cisco Systems

Cisco Systems, Inc. of San Jose, California, the global leader in networking for the Internet, prides itself on being an organization built on change, not stability—the very essence of being protean. The people we interviewed from Cisco will tell you that they don't have all the answers—they're still learning. Still, in the emerging field of how to manage acquisitions successfully, they stand out as a welcome early success story.

First, here are a few facts and figures to catch your attention. March 2000: Cisco became the largest company in the world in terms of market capitalization, moving ahead of GE and Microsoft. One share of Cisco stock purchased for $18 when it went public in February 1990 was worth $14,000 ten years later (the stock has split nine times).[16] More than 10 percent of Cisco's 23,000 employees are now stock-option millionaires. And Cisco has only recently set its sights on the huge consumer market; its previous focus was almost exclusively on the business-to-business arena.

Essentially, Cisco exists as a network structure, mirroring the Internet networking equipment it sells. In the year 2000, 84 percent of its sales will have been made over the World Wide Web, which is also a primary means of connection for job applicants, business partners, suppliers, and employees. It's not just technology but the fluid web of relationships that enables the company to maintain its competitive advantage. Cisco's chief networking relationships are with its customers, who are seen as partners in formulating strategy and who often provide the impetus and the inspiration for the company to make acquisitions.

Acquiring the Future

When Ford and Boeing, two leading customers, told Cisco CEO John T. Chambers that their future network needs could probably not be satisfied by Cisco, he made the company's first acquisition. In 1993, Cisco bought Crescendo Communications, a local-area-network switch maker. Ford and Boeing stayed on as customers, and a strategy was born. This acquisition was followed by fifty-four others as of May 2000, and that number changes monthly.[17]

Chambers, like many other successful acquirers today, sees acquisitions as a way of capturing intellectual assets and next-generation products, not manufacturing facilities or other "hard assets." He never forgets that "in a high-tech acquisition, you are really only acquiring people ... we are not acquiring current market share. We are acquiring futures."[18]

Cisco's acquisitions strategy has radically altered the company, which began as a manufacturer of switches and router devices. As one Wall Street analyst puts it, "Their acquisition strategies have allowed them to pull away from the rest of the pack."[19] Another Wall Streeter says, "Cisco was the first to identify opportunities in entering new markets via acquisitions. In my view, all the other companies followed its lead."[20] Over 25 percent of Cisco's current employees joined the company via an acquisition.

Since 1993, Cisco has bought more than fifty companies, typically smallish ones valued between $50 and $300 million.[21] Its purchase of Crescendo was followed by the equally successful acquisition of Grand Junction, a specialist in switching technology for low-end desktop computers, and Kalpana, also a manufacturer of switching products.

The motive behind most of these acquisitions is to close a gap in the knowledge or skills required to achieve Cisco's mission. Cisco wants to be number one in all the markets in which it competes. Whatever products and services their own R and D engineers cannot create quickly enough in-house, Cisco goes outside to buy.

Perhaps most notably, Cisco's leaders ensure the success of these purchases by focusing significant, dedicated resources on the task of successful integration. There are eleven full-time people, for example, whose sole work is integration of the human resources aspects of acquisitions around the world. Another group focuses on the structural integration of the businesses. The extent to which Cisco allocates resources specifically to the integration of new acquisitions is both impressive and unusual; Cisco's leaders believe this sort of investment is a cornerstone of their success.

A Culture of Acquisitions with a Shared Vision

Cisco also ensures that its corporate vision is consistently and coherently presented to the employees in all the companies under its corporate umbrella. Chambers's expression of that vision is simple: "We can change the way people live and work, play and learn." He envisions a time when "you are driving home from work and press a few icons on your car computer (which pops out of the dashboard at the press of a button) to turn on the heating or air-conditioning at home. Better heat up the oven, too."[22]

For Cisco, as for other successful acquirers, building a shared vision for the future is a key factor in its effectiveness. Even as the protean corporation is changing its shape constantly, a strong vision helps to keep its focus and identity intact. A compelling vision that the acquirer can communicate clearly provides a sense of unity and purpose that allows people on both sides of the acquisition to work together successfully toward a common goal.

Cisco first measures the success of each new acquisition in terms of employee retention. Mimi Gigoux is in charge of the human resources aspects of acquisition integration for Cisco (you'll be hearing from her a lot in this book). Gigoux reports that her performance is still measured on the retention rates of employees at Crescendo, its first acquisition, which was acquired before she even joined the company. Overall turnover in acquired companies is a miniscule 2.1 percent, compared with an industry average ten times greater. Cisco's acquisition success is also measured in terms of new product development and return on investment.

The emphasis on retention of talent has led to very healthy returns indeed. Broad-based option plans, personal contact with employees (despite the state-of-the-art computer networks, there remains an emphasis on face-to-face meetings), and a culture of open communication and egalitarianism have enabled Cisco to become a model for how to integrate new acquisitions and enlist the commitment of its newly acquired employees.

CISCO'S JOHN CHAMBERS
ON ACQUISITIONS

[Acquisitions] are a requirement, given how rapidly customer expectations change. The companies who emerge as industry leaders will be those who understand how to partner and those who understand how to acquire.

When we acquire a company, we aren't simply acquiring its current products; we're acquiring the next generation of products through its people. If ... all you are doing is buying the current research and the current market share, you're making a terrible investment....

This is a culture that accepts outsiders with the realization that brain power is what counts, and if you can get brain power that fits into your culture, that's how you win.

source: James Daly, "The Art of the Deal" (interview with John Chambers, CEO of Cisco Systems), *Business 2.0*, October 1999.

And Now for
the Bad News

Unfortunately, Cisco is more the exception than the rule. Research tells us that for every company that has been effective at using acquisitions to achieve its strategic and growth goals, there are two or three companies that have merged with far less success.

The numbers differ, depending on exactly what is measured in the various reports in the newspapers and business journals, but the message is the same. Most mergers are not fulfilling their promise. Most are not considered successful according to the criteria that were established at the outset. Most acquisitions fail.

One comprehensive study of corporate mergers showed that the profitability of acquired companies more often declined than increased.[23] Other studies cite similarly gloomy statistics: An analysis of more than 300 deals valued at over $500 million found, for example, that after three years, only 43 percent of the merged companies were outperforming their nonmerged peers in total shareholder return.[24] Larger deals performed even more poorly: Of deals valued at one-third or more of the acquiring company's annual revenue, fully three-fourths failed to create value.[25]

Sometimes, the acquirer may see the worth of its own company decline dramatically: When software manufacturer Adobe Systems bought Frame Technology, for example, the problems with its new acquisition drove Adobe's stock down by half within a few months of the purchase.[26]

In fact, the acquirer may not only lose money but may also see its excellent reputation sullied, as happened during Union Pacific's trouble-ridden acquisition of Southern Pacific and the Virgin Group's blundering takeover of portions of British Rail.

During 1996, Union Pacific lost the goodwill of its customers as a result of its problems integrating Southern Pacific's system with its own. Throughout the year, railcars were reported missing, rail depots were jammed, and finally total gridlock resulted from Houston to L.A.; hundreds of frustrated shippers incurred business losses. A group of shareholders even sued, claiming misrepresentation of the benefits of the merger.[27]

In the late 1990s, the rail industry mergers in the North American rail industry were so egregiously mismanaged that in March 2000, U.S. regulators imposed a fifteen-month moratorium on *all* rail mergers. The goal was to "provide an opportunity to formulate performance standards and prevent the kind of service interruptions that have plagued recent rail mergers."[28]

Similar problems arose with a rail merger in the United Kingdom. In 1997, the Virgin Group, led by flamboyant entrepreneur Richard Branson, took over all the cross-country and West Coast lines of the former British Rail. Virgin suddenly saw its relationship with the public sour due to the frequent delays and cancellations of the train service people depended on to get to work. *Business Week* reported that "Virgin has been plagued by embarrassing missteps and bad publicity"[29] as a result of the British Rail acquisition. In 1998, a Virgin executive admitted that "[t]he experience is damaging Richard and Virgin's reputation overall."[30] Two years later, a spokesman for Virgin said that they are "taking steps to meet the challenge and meet all the promises that Richard Branson made to the British people."[31]

Paying Lip Service
to Good Ideas

Leo Tolstoy wrote, "Happy families are all alike; every unhappy family is unhappy in its own way."[32] Like Tolstoy's unhappy families, every failed acquisition unhappy in its own way, too. The unique combination of circumstances, culture, personalities, and interactions will never be replicated anywhere else. But there are a number of common assumptions and early warning signs that can be discerned in many failed acquisitions. When we analyzed the myriad failures that are available for study, some definite patterns emerged.

As one software company executive who has been involved with dozens of acquisitions sees it, "A lot of lip service gets paid to good ideas, like taking enough time to do things right, or being sensitive to the people in the other company, who after all are the chief asset you're acquiring. But as a practical matter, most companies don't do what they say they believe in. And they pay the price."[33]

In the chapter that follows, we'll take a look at some of the most common reasons for merger failure—and then consider what can be done to avoid that all too frequent result.

2

WARNING SIGNS

Danger Ahead!

> *If you want a recipe for disaster, just mix a tablespoon of confidence with a tablespoon of ignorance and stir well.*
>
> **—Hollis Paine, *Walking the Talk***

There is certainly no single right way to integrate two organizations; there are, however, any number of wrong ways to do so. Having viewed, reviewed, and *endured* so many acquisitions over the last decade, people are beginning to recognize some early warning signs that may signal disaster ahead.

Watch out for these warning signs and phrases—they are often based on faulty assumptions, and the true meaning behind them is often obscured, though not always intentionally or consciously. Below is our list of the six top warning signs or phrases to watch out for—and an explanation of what they may really mean.

"It's a merger of equals."

This is one of the most common statements—the espoused rhetoric—that is used in the announcement that two companies will join forces. It reminds us of George Orwell's famous formulation: "All animals are equal, but some animals are more equal than others."[1]

In reality, over time, one company—its leaders, its culture, its way of operating—will generally win out. This does not mean that the new company cannot include the best of both previous ones and form its own culture. But attempting to manage an integration as a merger of equals is generally dysfunctional. Decisiveness is one key to realizing the value of an acquisition, and decisiveness is difficult to do by committee or co-CEOs.

Listen to Bill White, former CEO of Bell and Howell on the merger of equals he participated in: "It's a terrible idea. You're likely to end up with a power struggle that will divide the company. What I didn't realize then is that when you create a co-CEO structure, you are basically defying human nature. We polarized the company, and it was a disaster."[2]

When the CEOs from the two merging companies pronounce, "It's a merger of equals," it may mean one of several things. The first possibility is: "We're not being honest with you." Very often, the senior leaders involved in a deal recognize that one company and one leader will be dominant going forward. However, in an attempt to gain the acceptance of the senior executives and employees of the acquired organization, the deal will be announced as a merger of equals. Duties of the two CEOs are divvied up and obscured in a maze of responsibilities, but in private, both parties agree about who's really going to be running the show.

The real danger here is that false expectations are created, particularly among people in the acquired company. Look what happened with DaimlerChrysler: The morale problems in the U.S. organization were widely reported in the months after the deal. There was a dawning recognition and sense of betrayal among Chrysler employees that they had indeed been acquired and the company would be managed from Germany.

Semantics may play a pesky role here. One Chrysler executive who was pressed on the issue insisted, "I think it was true, it is true, and it will continue to be true that it's a merger of equals…. Remember that a merger of equals means that we brought two companies together with significant strengths, of almost equivalent size, strength, and profitability. But it's time to get on to the next phase of things."[3]

The next phase of things came as a considerable shock to many on the U.S. side. According to the *New York Times* four months after the merger, "American managers still at DaimlerChrysler also complain privately that more and more decisions are being made at Daimler's former headquarters in Stuttgart, Germany, even though Daimler-Chrysler officially has dual headquarters, there and in the Detroit area."[4] An auto-industry journalist commented, "Those who stay will have to live with the fact that what they thought was a friendly merger with Daimler-Benz was actually a takeover.... Nine of the 12 top jobs in the new company are held by Germans."[5]

Admittedly, the reaction would probably have been similar if this deal had originally been announced as a takeover. However, it was certainly compounded by a general feeling of distrust and disappointment that management had been less than honest in the initial announcement.

This distrust can also spread beyond the walls and halls of the acquired company into the communities that are affected. The NationsBank–Bank of America merger, which was touted as a merger of equals, sparked an outcry in San Francisco, as it became very clear that it was no such thing. This was "more a case of obliteration than integration," according to the *San Francisco Business Times*.[6] Promising one thing and delivering another in this and other deals helped Nations-Bank CEO Hugh McColl Jr. win the unenviable title of "number one merger partner to avoid" in a survey by *Bank Director* magazine.

Another possibility is that the leaders of the two companies actually do believe that they can manage the new entity as equals. This has not proven to be a workable assumption in most cases.

At the new Citigroup, the CEOs announced that they were going to share power equally. In January 1999, months after the spring 1998 merger, the *Economist* reported that "employees spend much time trying to work out whether Sandy Weill of Travelers or John Reed of Citicorp is top dog. The combined firm's troubles recently led to the loss of a high-flying manager, Jamie Dimon."[7] This example is supported by research that suggests that the stress for employees is greater when the roles and power relationships in a merger are unclear.[8]

In a speech to the Academy of Management in August 1999, John Reed talked about the difficulty of leading change under a co-CEO structure. "The Travelers people are ticked off that they did the merger, because clearly these Citi people are a bunch of idiots....The Citi people are equally annoyed. Sandy and I both have the problem that our 'children' look up to us as they never did before, and reject the other parent with equal vigor, saying 'Sandy wouldn't want to do this, so what do I care about what John wants." In March 2000, John Reed stepped down, nearly two years after the agreement to merge.

The fact is, in a true merger of equals, there would be nobody in charge—which would impede decisionmaking. Yes, responsibilities and accountabilities can be divided and clarified on both sides, so that such an arrangement is theoretically functional. However, when issues cannot be resolved at lower levels, someone—one person—needs to be responsible for making the final call. With two people at the top, there is likely to be more confusion and speculation about where the buck stops, wasting time and energy.

We'll stop short of saying that this kind of arrangement can never work. There are, however, few examples of CEOs who can truly make this kind of power sharing effective in reality and few organizations that have the high tolerance for ambiguity required in such cases.

"*We* bought *them*."

Another warning sign that a merger may be inclined to failure is when you start hearing variations on this theme in the hallways and cubicles of the acquiring company: "Now wait a minute, *we* bought *them*!"

Translation: "We're the conquerors; let them learn to do things our way." Or, "We're not listening and we're not learning." This is the arrogant acquirer syndrome in action: a sense of conquest and superiority that, if it goes unrecognized and unchecked, can wreck even the most promising acquisition.

This is big dog meets little dog. You can see this dynamic play out in people's body language. Go into a room with people from both sides on the day that the deal is announced. You'll see managers from the acquired company almost cowering. It's generally quite clear who are the victors and who are the vanquished; as the acquirers strut in, every movement suggests "Hey, let's pillage—*we* bought *them*!"

To a certain extent, a feeling of triumph on the part of the acquirer is inevitable. Every purchase of another company, particularly if it's a former competitor, as is often the case, is in some sense a conquest. This is particularly true when the acquired company was in financial trouble and had to be acquired.

But if such feelings are allowed to run rampant—if they are never dealt with or resolved—they will have multiplicative negative consequences. If the victor-vanquished mindset persists in the combined organization, real collaboration will be difficult. The acquirer will wind up with a group of demoralized acquired employees. The very talent it paid good money to obtain will no longer be functioning at anything like its former level (not to mention the possibility of mass emigration).

The conqueror's mindset generally carries with it an automatic assumption that the acquirer's practices, procedures, systems, and ways of doing business must be superior to those of the acquired ("After all, we must be smarter than they are—that's why we were able to buy them.") So the acquirer's processes are thus adopted throughout the new organization, and all the benefits that might have been realized from drawing on the acquired company's strengths or innovative approaches are in danger of being lost.

An employee of U.S. Robotics said of his company's acquisition by 3Com, "There was discussion at the time of the acquisition that 3Com and U.S. Robotics would compare how things were done in both companies and look for best practices and come up with a hybrid that was the best of both worlds. But the reality was that basically we were going to do it 3Com's way. It was hard on morale, it was hard on productivity."[9]

Examples abound of arrogant acquirers who were so sure their ways were best that they wound up getting rid of the very things about the acquired company that had given it its differential advantage. Novell, when buying the Word Perfect Corporation in 1994 for $1 billion, decided that its standards of customer service would prevail. Novell believed that Word Perfect had been excessive in its notions of what constituted good service to the users of its word-processing software and cutbacks could easily be made. But customers who had relied on the high level of support they got from WordPerfect staff deserted for Microsoft Word, and when Novell sold most of the WordPerfect product to Corel Corporation two years later, it was for about $185 million in cash and stock—a loss of 81.5 percent or $815 million!

As Glenn Goldman, a former merchant banker who has been responsible for overseeing two dozen acquisitions, reminds us, "No acquisition ever failed as a result of excess humility on the acquirer's part."[10]

ON DEALING WITH AN ARROGANT ACQUIRER

I thought to myself, who is this guy from Corporate who thinks that he's my boss? For the last twenty years, I've been the boss. Because he's at Corporate, he can send me a memo or an e-mail and say, "This is how we're going to be doing things around here from now on." And he thinks I'm just going to do it?

I wanted to say to him, "Do you realize I'm the guy who launched this business? Do you know how hard I worked *and am still working* to make it a success? And now *you're* telling me how we're going run it?" I don't think so.

I felt like a peasant in one of those war movies—you know the kind. The army moves in and they summon him to headquarters and tell him they want him to go clean the villa on the hill that the family he's always owed his allegiance to has just fled from. Or he's got to act as their servant from now on or hand over his prize pig or whatever. I couldn't believe it. I thought, "This can't be happening to me."

SOURCE: Interview with an entrepreneur whose firm was acquired, June 1999.

"Nothing will change."

When leaders use this phrase, often early in the deal-making process, it is usually an attempt to reduce the anxiety of those in the acquired company. Subtext: "We're either kidding or we're dummies."

The new company will always be different from the previous two: All acquisitions are based on the assumption that value will be created, and it's highly unlikely that value can be created without also creating change. In addition, there may always be further acquisitions and more changes down the road. That's not necessarily a bad thing. In this book, we'll talk a lot about change—about the protean environment, the protean organization, the kinds of changes that take place in two companies when they merge. For many people, change is something to be dreaded and resisted. And certainly it can be difficult. But it often has its rewards, too.

MORE THOUGHTS ABOUT THE ARROGANT ACQUIRER SYNDROME

They've acquired a lot of businesses. I've talked to some of the other people in the other companies they have acquired, and they're as frustrated as we are. Nobody's asking them anything; nobody comes and says, "Show me what you're doing and how you do it." I got this memo today saying, "From now on we'll do hair testing for pre-employment." Not "What are you doing now?" No dialogue, just do it. And the whole thing has been like that.

They think we're going to have all these great synergies, but they don't really understand the processes they're trying to merge, and they haven't asked the people who work here, "Why was that facility organized that way? What made you design the inventory system like that? Why do you sell from that facility to that region?"—that kind of thing. So some of what looks so great on paper, it's just not going to work. They're heading for some big shocks.

SOURCE: Interview with a human resources manager of a recently acquired company, May 1999.

That's why "nothing will change" is a dangerous form of wistfulness. Employees who resist the changes taking place and try to go on doing things the old way in the new environment are likely not only to be unhappy but to find themselves out of a job.

This is closely related to another warning phrase: "We love them just the way they are."

This statement by the head of the acquiring company may be followed by such phrases as "We're not going to interfere; we're going to respect their autonomy." This kind of talk reminds us of something Emerson once said: "The louder he talked of his honor, the faster we counted our spoons."[11]

When acquirers talk about respecting the autonomy of the acquired company and not interfering, what they often mean is "We love them just the way they are, and we're going to make them even better by making them just like us." It's hard not to wonder how long it will take for the next announcements to be handed down: "We're moving the acquired company's people into our corporate offices ...

we're consolidating the purchasing functions ... we're closing down some plants ... we've just accepted, with regret, the resignation of the CEO."

What has happened to change things? Often, the acquirer is really sincere about loving the company the way it is. That's why it was such an attractive acquisition candidate, after all. But the impulse to impose the acquirer's policies and procedures, to forget that there can be two good ways of doing something rather than just one (*our* way) becomes too strong for many people to resist.

Similarly, it can be more difficult and anxiety producing to manage another company "loosely"—to allow it its independence—than it is to assume control and create a clone of the acquiring firm. A significantly different approach to doing business on the part of the acquired firm can make the acquirer's senior executives nervous—they're ultimately accountable, after all.

One employee of a company that was recently taken over by a larger firm describes it like this:

In September, when they announced they'd bought the business, they said, "Things are not going to change. We bought a family-run business with competent management, and we like it that way." For the next few months, they're telling us that nothing is going to change and so on, and then suddenly we're in January, and things are really starting to tighten up.

In February, they come in here and tell us they're going to move their regional offices here. So I say to everyone, "Well, guys, that's not always bad. We're going to be right on the cutting edge." But I could feel the attitude of the buyer starting to change. Different things started to fly, and pretty soon their regional structure was overlaid on ours, and they brought in their regional salespeople and regional controllers and then everything had to be done their way, and the family was just being squeezed out. They weren't allowed to make the decisions any more. Meanwhile, the customers that had always done business with the family were going elsewhere."[12]

In the most extreme cases, the acquirers not only move in and start changing things; they decide, belatedly, that the acquired firm should be swallowed up into their own. Sometimes that can indeed be an appropriate form of integration. (The different possible forms an integration can take and when each form is appropriate will be considered in Chapter 7.)

Sometimes, too, it makes sense for an acquirer to begin by allowing the acquired company to operate independently, and then to increase the degree of integration. But acquirers who claimed they were going to let an acquired company go on as before often had good reasons for deciding that; a complete about-face on the issue after the fact suggests not a considered decision but a panic reaction, a control issue, or a false assumption that there's only one real way to merge: swallow 'em whole.

Whatever the acquirer's reasons, fixing what isn't broken—whether it entails an outright absorption of the acquired company or just changing things about it that were working fine—can be expected to have dual consequences. First, the morale of the acquired company plummets immediately; people's work suffers; if the situation continues, the best talent in the company will start heading for the exits. Second, even if the acquirer manages to hang onto the human resources of the acquired firm, it is likely to be losing much of what it bought the company for: the distinctive products/services/attributes/ways of doing things that made it so attractive in the first place. A great deal of value is lost in the pursuit of unnecessary consistency.

David Farber, now CFO of Magic Cinemas LLC, remembers that after his office-machine company was bought by a larger firm, the acquiring company insisted on replacing what he saw as a sophisticated, well-functioning operating style with their own more old-fashioned, lumbering, rigid way of doing things. The result? More than half the finance and administration people left, customers deserted in droves, and profits disappeared.[13]

Or look at AT&T's 1991 acquisition of NCR. AT&T admitted that it had failed to develop a successful computer business; this was a clearly stated strategy that followed the Ma Bell breakup in 1984. ("From the start," reported the *Economist*, "AT&T made a pig's ear out of the computer business.")[14] They bought NCR to learn the business from them, and then spent the next five years trying to make them just like AT&T.

The interesting thing about this failed merger was that the acquiring company, AT&T, had developed what might be considered a more "enlightened" culture and attempting to impose that culture caused great difficulties. Jerre Stead, the AT&T executive who was put in charge of NCR, was cited in our previous book, *The New Strategists*,[15] as a real pioneer in involving people at all levels in strategy making. In this case, however, the fit was not optimal. According to the same *Economist* article, Stead was "an AT&T man, and he was going to run the company the AT&T way. But the full gravity—and levity—of what that meant did not sink in until NCR's employees got new business cards. Employees were 'associates'; managers became 'coaches'; Mr. Stead was 'head coach.' Embarrassed executives had to print up a second batch of business cards with more traditional titles, for use outside the company."[16]

In 1996, the company that they had paid $7.5 billion for and spent more than $2 billion to integrate (renamed AT&T Global Information Solutions) was again on the block for about $4 billion. It was spun off; NCR's revenues for the first nine months of 1997 were $4.6 billion, and operating losses were $29 billion during that time.[17]

"It's a natural fit."

This phrase is used to describe to analysts and potential investors the rationale behind many an acquisition. There is nothing wrong with the phrase, per se. The strategic justification for an acquisition may be compelling and the logic impeccable, based on complementary strengths and the combination's ability to exploit emerging opportunities.

That doesn't mean, however, that the synergies that are alluded to so often in discussions of mergers will emerge effortlessly once the deal has gone through. It's dangerous to assume that any fit is "a natural," because such thinking can lead to complacency. Leaders who emphasize the natural fit may be sending an unintentional message that the integration will be easy, or they may be telegraphing that "we don't know what we're up against with this integration."

That's what happened when Quaker Oats bought Snapple on the assumption that Quaker could leverage its extensive distribution system to broaden the distribution of Snapple beverages. It soon became clear that the markets for Quaker's more mainstream products and the markets for Snapple were significantly different and a different distribution network was required. And Quaker paid heavily for its mistake.

Not only did the company lose a whopping $1.4 billion when, less than two and a half years after buying Snapple, it had to divest itself of its recent acquisition, but Quaker also lost a lot of face: The spectacular failure of its much-touted acquisition was widely publicized and written about in the business world.

In fact, even in successful mergers, the synergies that a company expects to achieve through an acquisition are often not the ones that wind up being important; they may never emerge at all. Very frequently, companies buy other companies in the expectation of being able to merge functions or processes that on closer analysis, prove to be wholly incompatible. These obstacles—the fact that one information technology system simply cannot interface with another, the fact that the sales processes and focuses of the two companies are radically different, the fact that the distribution system of the acquirer does not extend to the markets for the acquired company's products—only surface after the deal has gone through.

More frequently than is generally acknowledged—about two-thirds of the time, in our experience—it's the synergies no one anticipated, those that become apparent only once the integration is underway, that prove to be the most profitable over the long term. In most cases, synergies do not simply emerge because two companies' markets or products naturally complement one another. Synergies are usually the product of the kind of innovation and problem solving that can take place only as people within the two organizations grow to understand each other's strengths and talents and the ways in which they might complement each other.

Thus, another danger of looking on a merger as a natural fit is that once the leaders of the acquiring company get a fixed idea of what the synergies ought to be, they may stop looking for others. They may lose those unexpected opportunities that surface or are identified once people from the two companies start exchanging ideas and opinions on an ongoing basis.

Even if the anticipated synergies are enough in and of themselves to ensure the success of the merger, they will not materialize without an enormous expenditure of time, effort, and resources. You could say that a natural fit is like natural athletic talent: It requires unremitting hard work before it can blossom.

CREATING VALUE

We never said that two plus two would simply equal four. Success will be determined by execution, so it isn't going to happen overnight. But that's how value is created—by each party bringing something different to the table.

SOURCE: Dick Kovacevich, CEO of Norwest Corporation, on Norwest's merger with Wells Fargo and Company, as quoted by Karen Kahler Holliday, "Melding Opposites Model into a New Company Profile," *U.S. Banker* Vol. 109, Issue 2, February 1999, p. 43

"The integration plan has been finalized."

The good thing about this phrase is that it suggests that there is indeed a plan for the integration.

However, watch out for this statement if you hear it very early in the integration process; it may mean, "We don't know what we don't know." It has certain elements in common with the "natural fit" fallacy: It's a signal that there will be no room for synergies to evolve, that the integration process will not allow room for the unexpected, for adapting to new circumstances, opportunities, and ideas as they emerge.

In fact, no matter how careful the due diligence has been, there are often things the acquirer cannot find out about the company it is buying before the deal is concluded. In most cases, during the negotiation phase, much of the contact between the two organizations will be at a very senior level. Few companies that are candidates for acquisition will allow or are legally allowed to invite a potential acquirer to enter its offices, talk to its people, and find out all there is to know about things like its competitive strategies, its mode of working, and its R and D projects.

In many cases, the most that can really be hoped for at this stage is to get some general indication of how the other firm goes about things: what its values and its management philosophy are; how it sees itself; what its current direction is. The acquirer may be working more from clues than from a lot of definite information. Such a situation holds even truer when a competitor is the potential buyer and when an acquisition spans countries or continents, as it often does now. The real familiarity comes later. How, then, can an integration plan be mapped out step by step, when there are so many unknowns? It can't be.

Does that mean that the planning process should not be set in motion until after the deal has gone through? Absolutely not. Integration planning should begin well before the close of the deal. But there needs to be a built-in recognition that the plan will have to undergo many, many revisions as the integration process unfolds and unexpected contingencies and opportunities arise: Adaptability is the key to success.

Senior management will never be able to anticipate all the pitfalls, problems, and potential synergies that will become apparent over time. Any good integration plan needs to be based on that assumption; its design should be fluid enough to allow for what may feel like endless modification. In short, the plan, too, needs to be protean.

"We're buying them for their markets and their assets."

This seems to be business code for "We're taking their customer base and firing all their people." If you're in a company that is about to be acquired and you hear the acquirer say this, start working on your résumé.

This is a perfectly viable strategy when it's necessary. Sometimes, however regrettable it may be, it really is important and necessary to eliminate large numbers of positions and lay off many people after an acquisition. In an acquisition that seeks economies of scale in an industry that is consolidating, for example, this approach may be the only way to save the business and the jobs of the people who remain.

But it's very rare that acquirers really want to get rid of *everyone*. They may think that they'll skim off the cream; they plan to keep the people who are indispensable, who have special skills and knowledge that can help them exploit the resources of the company they've just bought. "We're gaining access to the some of the best minds in the business," acquirers boast, assuming that these people will want to work for them.

Often, however, these are the very people who choose to leave voluntarily, despite efforts to keep them; the company is left with people who have few other options. Issues related to relocation, title and role changes that feel like demotions, lack of respect for a new boss, and a belief that autonomy or career advancement will be more limited are common. Because people's knowledge and relationships are often high value assets, the loss of key players can derail the success of an acquisition, no matter how well intentioned the acquirer is.

In addition, large-scale layoffs can undermine the "survivors'" commitment and loyalty to the new organization. Even when staff reductions are handled well, they are almost guaranteed to sow fear, distrust, paranoia, and other counterproductive emotions.

One employee who saw his longtime boss squeezed out after an acquisition put it this way:

> Those guys [the acquirers] probably really shouldn't have made those commitments to people because they couldn't have been further from the truth. They weren't intentionally misleading. They treated him pretty fairly, but in the end, he had to fight. Everything we had here he was a part of, and now there's no place for him. I think most of the people here feel there *should have been* a place. Every time you have one of these people leave, you go back into that "two-week-gotta-start-looking" mentality. The "you're-next" mentality. You feel like you can't really believe anything you're hearing.[18]

In a tight job market, with many people taking early retirement (particularly when an acquisition is in the works), it can be hard to replace the people who have been let go. More than one acquirer that went in for whole-scale terminations has wound up having to hire back some of the very employees it had laid off.

Cisco Systems, the protean manufacturer of networking equipment, has what it calls the "Mario rule," named after Senior Vice President Mario Mazzola, the former CEO of its first acquisition, Crescendo Communications. The Mario rule is simple: No one in a newly acquired company can be fired without an okay from both Cisco's CEO and the CEO of the other company. Daniel Scheinman, Cisco's VP for legal and government affairs, puts it simply: "It buys the trust of the people."[19]

In fact, Cisco's John Chambers even extended that rule in the recent acquisition of the telecom-equipment start-up Cerent Corporation. Cerent's CEO, Carl Russo, initially balked at selling his company to Cisco, since he had ambitions to take his successful company public. But even when Chambers agreed to match Cerent's expected initial public offering (IPO) value, Russo was not satisfied. He was worried about his employees' job security. And so Chambers, in an unprecedented move, promised that all personnel decisions about Cerent's employees would be made jointly by himself and Russo—forever.[20]

Of course Cisco is in the enviable position of being the leader in a high-growth industry, and it acquires companies specifically to add their unique expertise to Cisco's lineup. Consolidation and the accompanying layoffs are simply not required and not part of the acquisition strategy.

We cited Cisco earlier as a model of a successful acquirer—as one of the organizations that has generally avoided the pitfalls listed above. In the chapter that follows, we'll be looking at how these companies approach the challenge of merging with another organization. Having laid out some of the possible wrong ways to go about it, we'll focus on the right ways—and on some best practices that most successful mergers seem to have in common.

3

STEERING CLEAR
OF DISASTER

Best Practices of
Successful Acquirers

*The art of progress is to preserve order amid change and to
preserve change amid order.*

—Alfred North Whitehead[1]

The business press is full of examples of how to merge two companies
poorly. Success stories are harder to come by.

However, in our experience with our clients and our research for
this book, we were able to identify a number of companies that are doing many things right with regard to merger integration. People involved in the process in all of these companies will tell you that they've
made mistakes. In fact, much of what they learned was derived from
past missteps. Lance Mitchell of PolyOne, a polymer technology and
services company that is the aggregate of a number of acquired businesses, puts it this way: "We are committed to making *new* mistakes."[2]

Obviously, there are hundreds of issues that need to be addressed
and hundreds of large and small decisions that need to be made in any
merger process. All of them require careful thought and attention. But

BEST PRACTICES

Determine the Degree of Integration Needed: Decide if it will be hands-off, bear hug, or a combination of the best of both

Develop a Systematic, Flexible Integration Process: Make it clear, replicable, and, at the same time, adapt and shape it

Avoid the Speed Trap: Be deliberate, decisive, and judicious, but avoid speediness for its own sake

Get People Talking: Face-to-face is best

Address the "Me" Issues: "What will happen to me?" is foremost on people's minds

Build in Two-Way Communication: Make communications complete, two-way, and true

Involve People at All Levels: People support what they helped to decide

what are the make-or-break issues—the decisions that will affect all the others? In this chapter, we'll look at several; these themes will be elaborated on in the rest of this book.

Best Practice: Determine the Degree of Integration Needed

In Chapter 2, we mentioned the tendency of some acquirers to promise autonomy and then erode it little by little. In other cases, an acquirer may announce from the outset its intention to fold the acquired company into its own. What is the right way to integrate a merged company? To what degree should the acquired company be integrated into the acquirer's?

Many acquirers don't realize that there is a choice to be made: They assume that there is only one way to integrate. Sometimes, it is a matter of their continuing to do whatever they have done in the past without questioning whether it's right for the new situation. If a company has had experience running wholly owned subsidiaries, senior managers may assume that this is the only possible approach. By contrast, sometimes new acquirers have the fixed notion that the only way to do things "thoroughly" and therefore correctly is to enfold the acquired company in a vast corporate bear hug.

In reality, there are a number of effective approaches to integration, depending on the characteristics of the two companies and the goals of the acquisition. Degrees of integration can be conceived of as a continuum that begins with alignment and moves through synthesis into consolidation (see Figure 3.1).

FIGURE 3.1   The Integration Strategy: Degrees of Integration

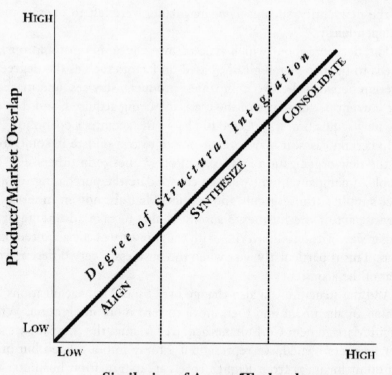

Similarity of Assets/Technology

A consolidation is the corporate bear hug referred to earlier: that is, the acquired company is wholly incorporated into the acquirer's organizational structure.

A synthesis, on the other hand, entails the integration of the acquired and acquiring companies into a new entity that capitalizes on the unique aspects of each. Typically, it involves a great deal more trading of staff and systems and processes than an alignment and is therefore a more complex management challenge.

Finally, an alignment calls for the acquired company to continue to operate within its own market environment, with its own business strategies, structure, systems, staff, and so on.

There may be elements of two or even all three structures in a single merger. In the original Time Warner merger, for example, back-office functions like printing were consolidated, cross-selling efforts were more typical of a synthesis, and at the same time, certain pieces of the new entity, such as *Time* magazine, were left to operate more independently.

The decision about which type of integration is most appropriate needs to be made strategically, based on factors such as the degree of overlap between the two companies' products, services, and markets; the current performance of the company being acquired; and the role the new acquisition is expected to play in the acquirer's portfolio.

In certain cases, it may be appropriate to consolidate in some areas of the new organization and to align or synthesize in others. For example, a company might want to consolidate the purchasing of indirect supplies (those goods and services that are not an inherent or direct part of the business's supply chain) to take advantage of its larger size, without interfering with the integrity of the acquired business. This is particularly wise when the business is very different from that of the acquirer.

And the structure can also change over time. Many acquisitions begin as an alignment and then move toward more integration. When Right Management Consultants acquired Manus, the company we and our partners owned, we represented a foray into a related but quite different business from Right's core career-transition business. We also had an established image among people who used our services. Therefore, for the first year, we operated very much as we always had and were careful to avoid unnecessary changes that might disrupt the culture or diffuse our focus. In the second year, we moved more toward a synthesis, coordinating our efforts and systems more closely with Right and with the other acquisitions that had been made since.

Because the choice of the degree of integration is so crucial to an acquisition's success, it's vital not to assume automatically that any one structure is the way to go. All alternatives should be considered carefully before the decision is made.

We will be focusing on the different approaches to degrees of integration and their implications for merger decisions in Chapter 7

Best Practice: Develop a Systematic, Flexible Integration Process

Another best practice involves using a clear, replicable process for capturing the value of an acquisition. Companies that are using acquisitions as a strategic lever are rarely making only a single deal; acquisitions are ongoing and often overlapping, with several happening at once and more to come.

Therefore, the most successful acquirers have developed a clear, logical, and replicable approach that they use to manage the entire process from initiation of the deal to the ongoing and longer-term development of the new organization post integration.

Cisco Systems has just such a deliberate and structured process, as does GE Capital. The process we outline later in this book draws on the best of these and on the work we've done with our clients, particularly PolyOne.

The process needs to be replicable—and it needs to be flexible, as well. This can be a tough balance to achieve, but it is critical. Even though Cisco, for example, is known for its consistent, well-documented process, flexibility is the key to its success. Every acquisition is different, and the process needs to be adapted to the unique needs of each one.

The integration process also needs to be malleable enough to allow for adaptation based on new discoveries. Sometimes, for example, the optimum type and degree of integration will become apparent only in the course of learning about the company being acquired. As more insight is gained into the company's processes, its strengths and weaknesses, its internal dynamics, and its potential synergies with the acquiring company, the appropriate degree and timeline for integration will become more apparent.

Best Practice:
Avoid the Speed Trap

One of the most common bits of merger advice—it has almost been accepted as a truism at this point—is: "Act quickly ... don't make people wait for decisions."

The push for speed comes from several very real forces. First, executives of the acquiring company know they have to show quickly that the merger was a good idea in the first place: It wasn't dilutive to earnings in the first year (unless of course this was accepted as a part of the deal), and the results that were promised really will be delivered.

Second, people in both organizations, and particularly in the acquired one, want to know as soon as possible what will happen to them. They are tolerating a lot of uncertainty, and they want to be relieved of that anxiety. "Put me out of my misery," the feeling goes. "If you're going to shoot me, shoot me now!" The underlying drive behind the push for speed is a very human discomfort with ambiguity. "Can't we just resolve this and get on with our lives?"

There may also be a benefit to consultants when companies try to integrate very quickly. If the people in the business are going to do the considerable and even overwhelming amount of work required to integrate successfully in a short time frame (on top of their real jobs), they will need a lot of consultants around to help. There may be, therefore, some pressure from those advisers as well.

Instead of assuming that faster is always better, however, leaders need to determine the optimal speed of integration and decisionmaking for their specific situation. It is true that acquisitions sometimes fail because decisions are not made in a timely way. There is great value in getting very clear about what decisions need to be made and in ensuring that they are made deliberately and decisively. Some decisions do indeed need to be made soon after the deal closes, if not before. Other decisions will require more deliberation, input, and involvement. But the key driver should be the desire to make the best decisions—not always the fastest ones.

Director of Human Resources Wendy R. Weidenbaum of Deutsche Bank, who was involved in the Deutsche Bank and Bankers Trust integration, puts it this way: "There are some things that you really should be fast on, like taking a look at what the platform is, where the market opportunities are, and what the strategy is. Then, you have to ask, 'If this is the platform, what are the possibilities? How can we structure this business; how can we structure that business?' They might all need different kinds of integration."[3]

Best Practice:
Get People Talking

We vividly remember sitting on a corporate jet with a group of senior executives who were preparing to meet with their counterparts at the former competitor they had just acquired. For half an hour, we listened to a series of exultant remarks about how they were taking the other guys' villages, had decimated their armies on the battlefield, and so on. Meanwhile, on our arrival at the other company's headquarters, we observed the obvious wariness, anxiety, and latent resentment on the part of the "conquered" ones at the meeting. Nobody who sat around that table could have had any doubt as to which group was the acquirer and which the acquired.

Half a year later, we were once again at a meeting with the same major players. This time, however, there was an almost palpable feeling of camaraderie and a sense of mutual respect; it was hard to remember that these people had hardly known each other, except as the enemy, a mere six months earlier. An issue arose concerning the inventory system that was to be used by the new entity; a senior vice president of the acquiring organization immediately suggested that they adopt the other firm's system, since, he said, "We all know it's more efficient than ours."

The integration of the acquired company into the acquirer had been proceeding relatively smoothly. Several of the anticipated synergies had already materialized: Customer service had improved, the company had established a stronger presence in some markets, and the profits were greater than the combined profits of the two organizations a year earlier. (This is a relatively rare occurrence within the first year, in our experience.)

It might be argued that the reason for the warmth and good feeling in the room was precisely the level of success that had already been achieved. But actually the process works two ways: In part, it was the camaraderie that had led to the successes.

What had happened in those six months to bring about the transformation in a group that had seemed to consist of victors and vanquished only a short time earlier?

In a nutshell, a management structure staffed with the best talent from both organizations was established very quickly, and those people had spent a lot of time together. At the urging of the acquirer's CEO, who had been through the process himself when his previous company was bought by a competitor, the new management team began by deciding how they would work together. That involved establishing some ground rules having to do with respecting each other's views, keeping the lines of communication open, and preventing conflicts from festering.

They had also spent time together informally, to talk about their companies and themselves, to get to know each other, and to tell stories about their experiences in their respective companies. They had gained insight into each other's ways of looking at things, and had examined the types of expertise and capability that each side brought to the table.

At the same time that the senior teams were meeting, systems people, human resources people, and marketing people from both companies were doing much the same thing—what one team member called "sniffing each other out."

At the initial meeting, an all-too-human arrogance prevailed on one side, and fear and resentment predominated on the other. At subsequent meetings, however, both the senior group and those less senior found themselves enjoying the novel, oddly pleasurable experience of talking to a competitor about how they *used* to see that competitor's operation. (This can be an especially interesting exercise with the newly joined sales forces.) They told each other what they had perceived as each other's weaknesses in various areas and how they had attempted to exploit those weaknesses; they could then talk about how those weaknesses might be eliminated in the new entity.

The big question was: "How can the strengths of the two companies as we have defined them be combined, and how can the weaknesses we have identified be eliminated?" How could the new entity they were designing find a way to take the best from each?

In the process of working out this and similar challenges, there was a great deal of laughter, as well as a great deal of brainstorming. And when it came time to implement the integration plans, solid ties had been established among many of the people on both sides.

Probably the most effective way to avoid the arrogant acquirer syndrome is to make sure that as many people as possible in the two organizations get to know each other as soon as possible. That means, of course, not simply sending in the acquirer's people to tell their counterparts in the acquired company what is expected of them but rather setting up the kinds of meetings in which there is a free exchange of opinions and ideas. In the course of doing real work, strategizing for the business, and solving current issues together, real breakthroughs can occur.

Having people sit down and talk to each other from the outset is not a cure-all, but it's certainly a start. It is harder for people to continue thinking of the other side as "them" once they really start getting to know people as individuals and talking to them on a daily basis.

Best Practice:
Address the "Me" Issues

In many cases, the employees of the company being acquired receive the news of the deal with trepidation, not the least of which is related to their own job security. Reorganizations and terminations accompany many acquisitions. Until their "me" issues are addressed— "What is going to happen to me? How will this affect me?"—people have a difficult time concentrating on anything else.

Affiliated Computer Services, based in Dallas, has a very active and effective acquisition strategy; we'll refer to the company several times later in the book. Executive Vice President and Chief Financial Officer Mark King of ACS has this to say about the importance of addressing people's "me" issues forthrightly:

The main thing is, you have got to be honest about what you are doing. About three years ago, we bought a company with 500 employees, and because it was in our exact line of business, we knew we were going to let forty to fifty people go. And we also knew that the number one fear people have is: "Am I going to keep my job or not?" So we bought the company on Friday morning and on Friday afternoon we laid off forty-five people and then we said to everybody else, "Okay, this is it. We made reductions. There will be no more reductions."

Some acquirers have two financial models, one to show people in the company that says they are not going to be cutting anybody, and another secret one that says what they're really going to do is cut 10 percent of the workforce and shut down two factories. And then what happens is, because they haven't been honest, they create distrust. We look the president of the company we're acquiring right in the eye and say, "This is it. There is no secret model. There will be no future layoffs. Nothing draconian is going to happen." And that way, when they are reporting to their people when we are not there, they can look them in the eye, too, and they'll have credibility. The worst thing that can happen is for people to be looking for you to lie. The second they catch you in a lie, the credibility is shot, and people are going to start leaving.[4]

As King notes, layoffs pose a particular challenge to acquirers, as people's jobs hang in the balance. Although staff reductions are always difficult, acquirers that handle them well have a better shot at a successful integration.

When Geon acquired Synergistics, a former competitor, it quickly became apparent that some plants would have to be closed down, since the two companies combined had more manufacturing capacity than would be needed for the foreseeable future. Geon dealt with the issue by communicating to the employees of both companies how things stood and assuring them that every effort would be made to find new jobs for those whose plants were closing.

Where that would not be possible, terminated employees would be given a fair and "more than competitive" severance package and help in finding new jobs. Although it was inevitably a painful experience for those who would no longer be employed by the company, the openness and sensitivity with which the matter was handled assured employees that management would be honest with them and that nothing would be done behind their backs.

Shortly after PaineWebber (now itself being acquired by UBS) announced that it had acquired Kidder Peabody in 1993, a decision was made that in each case of redundant responsibilities, the job would go to the person best qualified for it. "There was some consternation about that at PaineWebber," says Robert McKinney, the former CIO of PaineWebber, "but there were a lot of positions open, so it worked out well."[5]

In the end, about 95 percent of Kidder's systems people and 70 percent of their operations people were offered jobs with PaineWebber and were given an opportunity to meet the people they would be working for or with if they accepted. Most did.

FEAR IS NOT A GREAT CREATIVE FORCE

The one thing people are going to be thinking about from the minute they hear that the acquisition is going through is "What's going to happen to my job?" And until you answer that question for them—until you level with them, even if it's just to say, "Look, we don't know yet about every position, but we're pledged to treating everyone fairly and to helping people find new jobs if necessary"— they're going to find it hard to concentrate on anything else. They're going to be driven by fear, and fear is not a great creative force. It makes people's minds freeze up, just when you need their juices flowing.

SOURCE: Interview with a consultant, October 1999.

It is not always possible to answer people's "me" questions concerning job security and other critical matters immediately at the announcement of the deal. In these cases, when senior management doesn't know the answers yet, there can be a temptation to retreat into the executive suite and say nothing. A carefully thought-out communications plan that encourages interaction is another best practice, and an important one.

Best Practice: Build in Two-Way Communication

Useful though it is for people in the different departments of the two companies to sit down with their counterparts, there is also a need for a broad, ongoing program of *two-way* communication that spans various functions and levels.

In the past, corporate communications dealt mainly with creating carefully worded and packaged messages that were sent out to employees. Now, leading companies are emphasizing dialogue, face-to-face meetings, and listening, in addition to more traditional methods.

Generally, it pays to begin by offering at least the employees of the acquired company, who are more likely to feel anxious about the imminent change, a chance to air their concerns. These initial meetings also give them the chance to become acquainted with the organization that is going to have such a determining effect on their future.

Vice President of Corporate Services Don Decker of the Dana Corporation, a global leader in automotive components that has acquired over forty companies in the past eight years, is a firm believer in the following truism: "You cannot communicate too much. Until people are comfortable with the new environment, there should be constant, two-way communication."[6] Dana's policy has been to send first Decker and then Dana's chairman, Woody Morcott, who retired in 2000, on a visit to the acquired company within days of announcing the deal. Decker then pays a series of visits, both welcoming the acquired firm's people to Dana and answering any questions they may have.

Bill Hoenes, head of Dana's axle and brake business, formerly owned by Eaton Corporation, says: "The fact that Dana CEO Woody Morcott went to all the plants and facilities, including the ones in Europe, and talked personally to as many people as possible got things off on the right footing. And then each plant held an all-employee meeting, where people could ask Woody whatever questions they wanted. It was very very positive for everyone. He really welcomed everyone into the Dana family."[7]

Robert Grimes, an investment banker and venture capitalist who has been involved in a number of acquisitions with his clients, advises starting the communications process "as early as possible, as far down as possible, and make it as open as possible, to eliminate unnecessary concerns on the part of the people being acquired. Nothing taints the acquired company's view of the acquirer like being left in the dark for long periods."[8]

Of course, in an ideal world, this type of communication would eliminate all uncertainty for employees. But there will inevitably be times when people do need to be "left in the dark," for the simple reason that it is not yet clear what needs to be done or who will do what. In such cases, it is better for people to be told honestly that things are up in the air. When people are told nothing, as opposed to when they are told frankly that a decision has not yet been made, the rumors really start flying.

Part of living in a protean organization is living with uncertainty about the future. People who are relatively comfortable with ambiguity will not only weather a merger situation more easily, but they will be more valuable to many organizations experiencing rapid change.

Best Practice: Involve People at All Levels

Anyone who has been an eyewitness to a merger will attest to the intensity of emotion and human drama involved. There is no other corporate phenomenon that stirs up so many passions—a testament to the multilayered significance of such an event.

Leaders of companies that have been successful with acquisitions and integrations realize, first and foremost, that this is a process dependent on people and that these people may be at their most insecure and vulnerable. The best leaders remember that an acquisition will profoundly affect many people's lives—and that *these are the very people who will make or break the success of the merger.*

After the initial flurry of the announcement, ensuring employees' ongoing dedication to making the merger work can be even more challenging. If people feel that the decisions about their future and work are being handed down from on high by others they neither know nor trust, they are not likely to feel much enthusiasm for the integration process.

For that reason, a final best practice is to involve as many people as possible, as early as possible, in the planning process—and to involve people at all levels of *both companies.* One of the most telltale signs of an arrogant acquirer is that the merger process is planned almost exclusively, or at least predominantly, by the acquiring company (remember the warning sign: "*We* bought *them*"?)

Involvement of people from both sides can take many forms:

- Integration teams that focus on specific aspects of the integration, offering recommendations, developing, and often implementing integration plans
- Meetings and focus groups to provide feedback on these recommendations from other people across the company
- Widely disseminated real-time information: a constant flow of e-mails, electronic bulletin-board postings, and other interactive methods of communication that keep people informed of what is going on and solicit their input

The benefits of asking for people's advice and suggestions go well beyond making them feel part of the process. The real reason for reaching out to people at all levels of the organization has to do with arriving at those elusive synergies that every acquisition aims for and very few manage to achieve.

Widespread involvement was a key principle driving the integration of SonicAir, a service parts logistics provider acquired by United Parcel Service in 1995. David Abney, an executive who had been with UPS for twenty-five years, was appointed to head up SonicAir. Coming in from the new parent company, Abney was particularly aware of the need to involve SonicAir people at all levels. He remembers:

> Basically, what we did was involve people at the earliest stage possible. We said, "This is our challenge. How do you think we need to handle this?" Sometimes, we had an idea of which way we wanted to go. At other times, of course, as they always do, people would come up with things you hadn't thought of. People at all levels were involved at a very early stage. We also made sure that we had a spokesperson or someone who really owned the project who was considered one of them. We never used the UPS people to drive major changes. It was always done from within the group.[9]

Getting to synergies has at least as much to do with mutual problem solving and brainstorming as with inherent strategic potential. Thus, it really is crucial to involve enough people, from all different functions and levels of both companies, to allow these unplanned synergies to emerge—especially if the planned ones have turned out to be elusive.

We recently spoke with an executive at a hotel chain that had been acquired by a larger chain; the acquirer had confidently predicted that vast savings could be achieved by consolidating the reservations systems and sales forces of the two companies. It then turned out that the reservation systems were simply not technologically compatible. In addition, neither sales force was skilled at the kind of selling the other one did: Since one chain consisted of franchises managed for their owners and the other was centrally managed, the kind of selling required was completely different. The expected synergies related to cross-selling never materialized.

The merger might have turned out an embarrassing failure—except that executives from the acquiring company made a discovery, almost

INVOLVING PEOPLE FROM BOTH COMPANIES

The big plus of having integration teams that are fifty-fifty—composed of people from both companies—is that you get to build relationships with the people with whom you are going to be working in the future. You establish a means of communication and an understanding of each other and of why each company has some of the programs and systems it has.

SOURCE: Interview with Vice President, Workforce Effectiveness, and Co-chair of the Human Resources Integration Team Marsha Cameron of GTE, December 1999.

by accident. In the course of what they had expected to be casual get-acquainted meetings with people in the company they'd acquired, they learned that the leaders of the acquired chain had a positive genius for managing overhead. They turned over the management of one of their other recent purchases to their newest acquisition and saw indirect expenses in that chain reduced by 60 percent in just one year.[10]

Of course, there is no way to ensure that real synergies will surface, no matter how many meetings are held and how many people are involved in the process. But there is one way to ensure that synergies will certainly *not* emerge, and that is if the only people sitting down to discuss the merger are the senior executives of the two companies. Synergies will likewise remain dormant if the involvement of the "masses" is confined to a single meeting at which the CEO of the acquirer welcomes the employees of the acquired company. Those measures, effective though they can be, are merely first steps. What is required afterward is a lot of patient, systematic work and the allocation of considerable resources.

The GTE–Bell Atlantic integration (renamed Verizon), for example, which finally closed in June 2000, was based on the recommendations of myriad teams and subteams made up of equal numbers of people from both companies. In human resources (HR) alone, there were ten teams; each was assigned to develop integration plans for a specific HR area such as staffing, compensation, labor, or benefits. A team responsible for the overall human resources integration coordinated and guided the efforts of the subteams.

During the extended two-year waiting period, these teams met on a regular basis to develop HR plans and recommendations for the new entity (it had not yet even been named, so they referred to it as the often encountered "Newco"). They learned about each other's ways of doing things, and they discussed what they might change about their own current systems, given the opportunity to reinvent them. The goal was to find and build upon the best combination of the two companies' approaches.

Not Just How, but Why?

The foundation for all of these best practices is a clear sense on both sides of the negotiation table of exactly why the marriage makes sense in the first place. In the next chapter, we'll look at what goes into the decision to acquire or be acquired: Given the difficulties of merging well, what are the strategically sound reasons for doing so? When does it make sense, and why? And how does the deal making—the mating dance, if you will—happen?

4

THE MATING
DANCE

From Selection of Partner to
Announcement of Intent to Merge

*The thrill of the chase blinds the pursuer to the consequences of
the catch.*[1]

—Warren Buffett

As the title of this book implies, our focus is primarily on what happens "the morning after" the deal is announced. However, the post-announcement work to be done depends on what has gone before, and decisions that are made in the pre-deal mating dance will have significant impact on the likelihood of successfully merging the two companies. In this chapter, we examine what drives a deal from the perspective of both the acquirer and the acquired and what needs to be done during the deal process to make integration happen more smoothly.

Why Bother?

Given the rather dismal track record of most mergers and the negative impact that they have had on many businesses and people's lives, it is legitimate to ask, "Why bother?" That's like asking why people still get married when so many marriages end in divorce. In both cases, there are some very powerful human motivations behind the decision and a tendency to underestimate the amount of work that will be required to make the union succeed in the long run.

In Chapter 1, we talked about some of the driving forces behind the recent acquisitions boom. While these macro trends are pushing companies in many industries to join forces, the decision to acquire or be acquired is always made on an individual, case-by-case basis. A sound decision is rooted in the specific mission, strategies, and situation of the companies involved.

What kinds of objectives can be met through acquisition, and which are best pursued in another way? A lot of unnecessary pain, effort, and expense might be spared if those questions were asked and answered objectively every time a company was considering acquiring or being acquired.

Many explanations are given for why two companies should merge. There is, however, only one good reason for doing so: The acquisition will add value beyond what each entity would produce separately. *Acquisitions are strategic initiatives undertaken to create value in a market and realize competitive advantage.*

Why Buy?

SIZE MATTERS

As we discussed in Chapter 1, the rationale behind many acquisitions is that size matters. Being bigger offers opportunities and advantages that are unavailable to smaller companies. And the quickest way to get bigger is to buy.

For manufacturing companies in particular, the "bigger is better" rationale for making merger deals is often strategically sound. Producing a greater volume of product using the same asset base or the same volume with fewer resources means a lower cost per unit, which is often critical to market leadership.

Companies that make more product can also demand lower prices from their suppliers—they have more purchasing and negotiating power. In addition, if distribution costs are a substantial percentage of the cost of sales, moving more units through the distribution system helps to leverage fixed costs. For industries such as lodging and transportation, which have other high fixed costs, being bigger means that they can funnel greater numbers of customers through the system and increase the likelihood of being able to serve customers wherever they are.

And for makers of automobiles, integrated circuits, or pharmaceuticals, mammoth investments in research and development are required. Bigger companies can invest more.

Adding Value

But size on its own doesn't always translate into adding value. There are two major ways in which acquiring another company can add value.

Improved Efficiency.   The acquisition will allow the company to serve its current customers and markets more efficiently. An acquisition with this aim is based on the bet that the combined entity can produce an equivalent level of output using fewer resources or more output with the current resource allocations. The goal—think of the Exxon-Mobil merger—is to achieve higher levels of productivity through economies of scale. As a company does more of something, it (theoretically at least) learns to do it better and more efficiently.

Increased Scope.   The acquisition will allow the company to grow by extending its scope into new markets, customers, products, and services. This kind of acquisition brings the ability to see more broadly into more market areas, to spot emerging needs sooner, to take existing products into new arenas, and to create new product and service offerings. When MetLife, for example, acquired New England Financial in 1996, it was essentially acquiring a group of agencies with the skills and contacts to service individuals with high net worth. This market was an addition to MetLife's traditional focus on life insurance for the mass middle market.

In areas where internal development will be too slow, where there is literally no way to build the capability in time to respond to market changes and demands, acquiring other companies with the required talent and resources makes particular sense. Cisco is one of many high-tech companies that has acquired the technological talent it

needed to remain competitive through a consistent program of acquisitions; others in the high-tech area that have pursued the acquisitions
route include Microsoft, Netscape, 3Com and America Online. The
goal of AOL's acquisition of Time Warner was to marry technology
with content. "Technology companies have had a go at making content in the past," according to the *Economist*, "and found it surprisingly
difficult.... Creative stuff, it turns out, is tough to create."[2]

Access to specialized technologies and specialized talent that may be
required to meet market demands; access to global markets that might
be too costly or too risky to penetrate from scratch; the expansion of
product or service offerings: any or all of these goals can be achieved
through acquisition—at least in theory.

Sometimes, there is an additional factor at work: the desire to prevent a competitor from making the same move. It is not unheard of for
companies to acquire assets that could give their rivals a competitive
advantage. This is a somewhat risky strategy, based as it is on *predictions* of competitors' intentions and possible synergies.

Or a company may wish to acquire a supplier of the raw materials it
requires to manufacture its own products; this kind of back integration
can provide a cost-effective and secure supply that may not be available through any other means.

Why Sell?

And what about the other side? To begin with, there are the obvious
financial motivations—enrichment of shareholders, of the owner or
CEO, and sometimes of other senior managers and employees of the
acquired company. This is a driving factor that can't be minimized. A
recent issue of *Fast Company* featured the trend toward creating a company with the sole intent of selling it; the cover page caption read:
"Built to Flip."

There are also some more strategic reasons that leaders of a company may choose the acquisition route. These reasons often resemble
those of acquirers: accessing the advantages of size, creating efficiencies, or expanding the company's scope. In many instances, acquisition
is seen as a way to take advantage of resources that a smaller company
may simply not be able to muster on its own.

A company may have a product that could be very successful with a
more established distribution network. Another may be hampered by

the inability to engage in large-scale product development because of lack of sufficient funding; its leaders may be looking for an infusion of capital from an acquirer or access to that acquirer's distribution or sales network.

Similarly, a medium-sized company that lacks leverage with suppliers, that is finding it difficult to compete with larger organizations capable of negotiating more favorable terms, may regard being acquired as an opportunity to cut the cost of its raw materials and meet its competitors on a level playing field.

A financial services business might hope to reduce its cost of capital. Or the chance of gaining access to new technology and know-how may be a factor; small companies that cannot take advantage of the opportunities presented by new technologies as well as their larger competitors will increasingly be at a disadvantage.

Sometimes, the decision to sell is not much of a decision at all. This is certainly the case with hostile takeovers, which are expected to become more frequent, especially in Europe. In other cases, the business is in crisis and will not survive on its own. This was the case late in 1999 when General American Insurance Company suddenly found itself on the verge of financial collapse and quickly engineered the sale of the company, ultimately to MetLife. Bruce Brodie, CIO of General American, recalls, "We realized very quickly that even assuming the company survived, it would be permanently impaired, and so we had to sell the company to a strong player."[3]

Getting Clear About the Goal

Whether it's a matter of acquiring or of being acquired, it is vital for senior leaders and the team responsible for the deal to spend the time clarifying the strategic rationale for the decision. How would the acquisition help to meet the company's specific strategic goals? Building the business case for the acquisition involves answering such questions as these:

- What businesses are we in now? What businesses do we want to be in?
- What do we hope to gain? Which of our strategic aims do we hope to further through acquisition?
- How would an acquisition of this nature add value?

Although these seem to be fairly obvious questions, senior management teams can often assume that they are in agreement without really confirming that this is indeed true. Time spent crafting the answers to these questions is time well spent.

Once the goal is clarified, it's also worth spending some time thinking about the consequences of reaching that goal. What is the likely impact on shareholders and other stakeholders? What would an acquisition of this kind do to the industry? How might competitors and customers react? An acquisition that may spark a major market war in what is now a relatively stable industry is a scenario that needs to be anticipated and thoroughly assessed.

On Buying a Horse
When You Really Needed a Cow

Having a well-defined strategic goal also makes it much easier to evaluate various possible candidates: If members of a deal team know precisely what the goal is, they can do a better assessment of the alternatives.

It is not unusual for the acquirer to discover belatedly that the acquired firm, however excellent an organization, isn't really what was needed. The company went and bought itself a wonderful horse, when it actually would have been better off with a cow. When Sears, for example, decided to add financial services to its offerings, decisionmakers overlooked the fact that customers who go out to make hardware purchases do not necessarily want to buy investment products on the same shopping trip.

By the same token, leaders of the acquired company, having decided to sell in order to gain access to financial assets, may discover too late that the acquirer does not have the other assets required to maximize its potential. The acquirer may lack the technological expertise or the distribution system or the market knowledge required to add value. Or the assets the acquired company expected may not actually be made available or may not be what they appeared to be.

A company's leaders might have hoped that being acquired would give them access to a global distribution system, for example, only to discover that the acquirer's customer base or sales model was not in fact a good fit for the acquired company's products. We ran into this very issue, frankly, when we sold our high-end consulting business to Right Management Consultants in 1997.

Our firm, Manus, had spent more than a decade developing a number of state-of-the-art products such as 360-degree feedback instruments and business simulations. But we lacked a nationwide, not to mention global, presence and distribution system. Right, with more than 200 offices around the globe, seemed to be a good fit. Its core business was career transition (formerly known as outplacement), and the buyers of its services are generally high-level human resources people.

Soon after the deal was sealed, we began to learn that the expected synergies would have a lot more difficulty emerging than we had hoped. First of all, the career transition business operates under a different model than the consulting business. It's a quick-response, price-driven business.

Consulting, at least the way we had always approached it, is a more value-driven, specialty business. For many engagements, we are hired without a request for proposal. Our sales cycles are longer, and the sale is more complex. Our buyers are quite frequently line managers. When clients are in the human resources function, they are not generally the same people that Right's salespeople sell to.

Luckily, with some adjustments and a lot of hard work and cooperation, synergies did begin to emerge, and Right's excellent sales force helped to generate a significant amount of new business, even in the first year. But we admit that we could have done a much better job of understanding the differences between our business model and Right's much earlier in the process.

That said, it is important to remember that when the evaluation criteria are unclear, the acquisition may prove to be a disaster for both companies, adding value to neither. Both the would-be acquirer and the acquisition candidate need to ask themselves what it will take to develop the potential and whether those resources are in place on both sides.

For the acquirer, the process of evaluating candidates for acquisition should always involve an internal evaluation as well; after asking "How can this organization add value for us?" the next questions need to be: "What do we bring to the party? What sort of resources will it take to add value to this organization, and do we have those resources in place?"

Building the Ideal Candidate Profile

Apart from the most basic gauges of attractiveness such as financial soundness and potential availability, there is no single "ideal" candidate profile for all acquisition scenarios. Every acquirer needs to develop a list of mandatory and desired criteria based on the specific strategic rationale and the particular needs and resources of the company. These, however, are some general questions that management teams can ask to begin to identify the most important qualities, competencies, and assets to look for in a candidate:

- What technological, operational, and intellectual assets are we hoping to acquire? Why are they important to us?
- What new markets, if any, do we hope to access through acquisition? Define these either geographically or in terms of customer groups.
- What categories of new products, if any, are we interested in acquiring? Do we want to offer these products to our existing customers or enter new markets with them?
- If economies of scale are part of the strategy, what factors (i.e., degree of overlap among products, manufacturing processes, distribution systems) will allow us to achieve them?
- What types of potential synergy related to size, efficiency, or scope are we hoping to achieve, and in what areas? What must the other company be able to offer if we are to achieve those synergies?
- What kind of company culture would be the best fit with ours?

A list of desirable assets, customer groups, product types, geographic locations, and other such criteria will lead to the development of a profile of the kind of company that will be sought. Other criteria might involve competitive position:

- Who are the candidate's chief competitors in the segment or industry in which they operate?
- What are their respective market shares?
- Which, if any company, is the price leader, and what makes this position or power possible?

- How do the candidate's product or service lines compare to those of its competitors in both breadth and quality?

Similarly, a company that is considering being acquired should develop a set of criteria for evaluating potential buyers. These criteria will usually focus on the types of assets, resources, or markets the company is hoping to gain access to. Other considerations include the kind of company culture that the acquirer has developed, the degree of autonomy the seller wants after the deal (if the seller plans to stay), and how the buyer is likely to treat the people in the acquired company.

Lev Volfstun, who sold his company, Lightspeed International, to Cisco, says that the entrepreneurial culture and freedom to continue to run the business as he saw fit was a key consideration in his decision to sell:

> Cisco has a tradition of acquiring many companies and maintaining them as autonomous business units. Cisco gives them a lot of freedom to grow their market and maintain their individuality and entrepreneurship. If you look at 99 percent of the acquisitions Cisco has made, you can look inside the company today and identify them as a specific business unit—a specific entity that continues pursuing its goals and strategies.[4]

The decision to sell is important and often emotionally charged, especially if the executive plans to remain with the new company. It is very difficult for many entrepreneurs to work for someone else; no matter how good a manager or leader the new boss is, he or she will still be a boss. Even in a company such as Cisco, Volfstun reminds us, "There are still obligations. There are still politics between business units, and they do compete when some products overlap. This climate requires some maneuvering, selling, agreeing, and influencing. I am a lot more straightforward. I like to control what I do. Running a start-up is a lot easier for my personality."[5]

One of the things Volfstun did before making his decision was to talk with the other companies that had previously been acquired by Cisco. Their positive experiences, along with a strong strategic rationale for the deal, led to his decision to sell.

SELLING THE SELLER
ON THE IDEA

We were the buyers, but it also worked the other way around. The seller had to be convinced that the right people were buying the company. The CEO had to trust me enough to want to see his brainchild, the fruits of thirty years of his labor and the labor of his people, handed over to us.

Often, the first thing the seller wanted to be sure of was would we respect their people? Would we keep them on, would we listen to them, would we have respect for the way they did things, and understand why they conducted business the way they did?

And then they wanted to know just what we could do for the company. Could we grow it without losing what had made it special? Would we put their resources at the company's disposal? Our technology expertise? Our sales network? Our R and D facilities? Were we going to nurture their baby? They had to look at the future and say, "What's going to happen to it when I'm not around any longer?" And they wanted to make sure it would be in good hands.

You can't get guarantees on everything. So the bottom line was, did they trust us? Did they think we were sincere about what we planned to do?

SOURCE: Interview with Bill Patient, former Chairman and CEO of Geon, September 1999.

Narrowing the Field:
Identifying Specific Candidates

Developing a profile of the "ideal" company to buy or sell to is a good place to start. This is, in essence, a wish list, and it is unlikely that any candidate will match all of the desired characteristics. Still, having an agreed-upon profile makes it easier to start identifying and evaluating likely candidates.

At this stage, before much access can generally be expected to the company itself, information on candidates often comes from people's prior knowledge of the industry and its players. It can also come from knowledgeable acquaintances, such as mutual customers or industry colleagues who can be trusted to keep inquiries confidential. Other avenues include public information sources like annual reports and the Internet, which is an invaluable tool in the acquisitions search.

WEB SITES OFFERING COMPANY INFORMATION

<http://www.annualreportservice.com> for links to on-line versions of annual reports

<http://www.businessweek.com> for business news, company profiles

<http://www.dowjones.com> for financial news, resources

<]http://www.dunandbradstreet.com> for financial information

<http://www.fortune.com> for business news, company profiles

<http://www.freeedgar.com> for SEC EDGAR filings

<http://finance.yahoo.com> for a wealth of research information

<http://www.hoovers.com> for company profiles

<http://www.integrainfo.com> for information on *private* companies

<http://www.moodys.com> for financial information, ratings

<http://www.schwab.com> for Charles Schwab site, company research

<http://www.vaultreports.com> for insider company profiles and message boards

<http://www.wsj.com> for *Wall Street Journal* on-line

In addition, you may want to access proprietary databases: Lexis/Nexis, Academic Universe, and ABI/Inform (university libraries are likely to subscribe).

NOTE: Some of these web sites charge for their services.

In many cases, even public information along with a certain amount of industry or company familiarity is enough to give evaluators a preliminary sense of the value range of a company. Firsthand information from people on the scene, however, is crucial to gaining a thorough understanding of the context in which the business operates and the specific circumstances and characteristics that make it unique. No acquisition decision should be finalized without such information.

Once there are sufficient data to evaluate the candidates according to the criteria established, answering the following questions can be useful in deciding whether a candidate is worth pursuing further:

1. How will *this* company help us to meet our broad strategic objectives and any specific strategic goal this acquisition is intended to help us attain?
2. What do this company's strengths and weaknesses appear to be?
3. Are we able to capitalize on the apparent strengths of the candidate? What resources do we have that will make this possible?
4. How can we add value to this company?
5. What are the synergies we intend to capture?
6. To what extent do the culture and operating philosophies of this company appear to be compatible with our own?

Clarifying Roles in the Deal Process

Evaluating candidates for acquisition or potential buyers can be extremely time-consuming. In addition to gathering information from the sources discussed above, it also often involves visiting the facilities of serious prospects. Particularly in the case of cross-border acquisitions, a great deal of travel may be called for.

If the roles in this stage of the process are not already well defined (for example, in an established acquisition deal unit), it is important to be explicit about just who will assume what roles and responsibilities in the evaluation process. Who will generate the list of potential candidates? Who will be involved in assessing the most promising candidates? Who will make the final call?

While this would appear to be a straightforward role clarity issue, it is, predictably perhaps, political in many organizations. Should line management in a specific business unit be involved in identifying and evaluating relevant candidates? What is the optimal role for functions such as human resources and information technology at this point in the game? As acquisitions become more and more central to companies' strategic plans, the stakes rise as to who should be involved, how, and how early.

However the roles are assigned, it is crucial to ensure that the resources are in place and that sufficient time is allocated to pursue the evaluation process thoroughly and effectively. Many companies have found that having specific people whose sole job is to spearhead the acquisition effort at this point in the process can make a huge difference, especially in cases where a number of prospects, countries, and locations need to be investigated.

At the former Honeywell, Inc., which merged with Allied Signal in 1999 to form Honeywell International, each business unit had a strategic planner who presented candidates for acquisition to a management committee that met twice a month. Once the decision was made to follow up with the candidate, the committee took over the process, but the person who made the original proposal and the head of the related business unit were consulted and informed throughout the process.

Many companies that are engaging in a long-term program of acquisitions have permanently assigned people to the task of hunting out and evaluating candidates. Often, these people have longtime industry experience and are familiar with a number of potential acquisitions.

In this way, a formal search-and-evaluation process can be supplemented by an ongoing policy of "keeping one's eyes open" for good candidates through reading the trade press or having casual conversations with industry insiders. It can mean being attuned to the suggestion that John Doe up in Milwaukee might be ready to sell his button company and devote himself to his golf game. Or it can mean taking the initiative and approaching a familiar company with the proposal when the time is right.

It's important not to delegate the candidate search work exclusively to one person, however, or even to one department, especially in a large company with many divisions. People in the business units will often have the most accurate and up-to-date information about what's going on with their industry segments, and their knowledge should be tapped.

Whether the route to deciding on good potential candidates involves a formal search-and-evaluation process, the input of investment bankers, or simply word of mouth, the team involved will begin to focus on a candidate or candidates that seem particularly attractive. The time has come to make that first, exploratory approach. At this stage, the acquisitions game may take on the tone of a new romance.

The Pick-Up Line: Making the First Approach

The story has it that the Time-Warner mega-deal was born the day *Time* president Nick Nicholas found himself dismissed early from jury duty. He ducked into a phone booth in the courthouse lobby to see if Warner CEO Steve Ross would have any time free that afternoon "to discuss a couple of things."[6]

Although many people tend to think that acquisitions are the province of gray-suited investment bankers sitting around vast polished tables in wood-paneled conference rooms, the initial approach is often quite casual, especially when the parties know one another already.

A CEO may phone another CEO and say, "I'm working on some new ideas I think you might be interested in hearing about" or "I've been made aware of some opportunities that you should know about. Can we get together to discuss them?"

Alternatively, a member of the acquirer's board who is acquainted with someone high up at the candidate company might be asked to make the approach. If the acquirer wants to remain anonymous at this point, an investment banker or other third party might make the initial contact.

In all cases, the first meeting is likely to be a rather secretive matter. If the CEOs are getting together, an inconspicuous meeting place will probably be suggested, such as a private hotel room or an out-of-the-way restaurant.

In the interest of secrecy, later meetings may even take place at the CEOs' homes. This was reportedly the case with Lodewikj de Vink and John Stafford, the chairmen of Warner-Lambert and American Home Products, as they were hammering out a proposed merger between their two companies. (Pfizer later interrupted this deal with a surprise bid. According to *Institutional Investor*, the joint marketing arrangement between Pfizer and Warner-Lambert for the cholesterol-lowering drug Lipitor included a "standstill" agreement that stopped Pfizer from making a play for Warner-Lambert unless another takeover was launched.)[7]

Wherever these initial discussions take place, there are usually several more private meetings to discuss the idea before the full management teams and the boards of directors are informed.

The Flirtation

If the relationship gets to this point, when both sides have expressed interest and the discussions are proceeding, everything is likely to look rosy. However, taking a romantic view of the acquisition can sometimes lead to false expectations and resentment later. The company hoping to be acquired may present itself in the most favorable possible light and downplay any possible sources of problems. The would-be acquirer may make promises that it may not be possible or strategically wise to fulfill later. This is the time when promises "not to change a thing" are most likely to be made.

Glenn Goldman, who oversaw dozens of acquisitions during his tenure as co-president of a merchant bank, says that when he sees two companies in the first flush of having "found" each other, it reminds him of a beer-enhanced late-night barroom conversation between new friends. With hazy goodwill, A turns to B and says, "Hey, man, I love you, ya know?" They are totally sincere at that particular moment, but the sentiment may not always outlast the hangover the next morning.[8]

How *should* the courtship be conducted, then? It is important for people on both sides to make clear right from the beginning what is most important to them—what is negotiable and what is not. It's natural but often fatal to avoid conflict by saying "We'll work it out later" rather than facing the obstacles from the outset. It's much better to acknowledge and thrash through the conflict early on and even to have the courage to walk away from the deal than it is to plow on in the face of a growing sense that something is amiss.

Of course, there are many things that *can* and should be worked out later, when more is known. For example, this is not the time to settle the question of whose inventory system will be adopted or whose supplier should be used to provide a given material. But the major issues, like the respective valuations of each business, who will have authority over whom, and how decisions will be made—the things that are really important to the leader of each organization—should be worked out now, not later.

Anticipating Possible Synergies

As should be clear by now, we do not generally feel that it is useful for leaders to settle too early on a definitive list of expected synergies. People involved early in the deal process are usually at senior levels of the organization and may be the furthest removed from certain nitty-gritty obstacles. These may include incompatible computer systems, for example, or differing needs of various market segments. The two companies may have developed different kinds of selling relationships, a longer versus a shorter sales cycle, or "redundant" products that are not really interchangeable in the eyes of the customer. All of these factors, which are extremely difficult to assess early in the deal process, will significantly affect the ability to realize synergies.

On the other hand, leaders have to start somewhere in the quest for synergies. At this stage, it may be useful to try, at least, to imagine what the synergies between the two companies might be. Like scientists working from a hypothesis, a list of possible synergies will at least give people something to react to and work with if and when the time comes for members of the two organizations to sit down together and thrash out integration plans.

At this stage, it's important not to start thinking of any list of potential synergies as being carved in stone. In the initial excitement of imagining all the wonderful things that could happen, it's easy to forget that what looks fantastic on lined yellow paper will need to be carried out by people—people who don't really know each other.

In drawing up a list of anticipated synergies, it is common for leaders to focus *either* on synergies of scope such as increased market scope or product development *or* on efficiency synergies such as cost reductions. A more fruitful approach is to consider synergies of both sorts. If nothing else, this exercise will at least serve as a reminder that both are possible.

Initial Due Diligence

"Due diligence" is a business review of a target company that is used to determine if the proposed transaction should be completed.[9] In most cases, due diligence begins as the acquirer is deciding whether or not to buy a candidate, and it continues more extensively between announcement of the intent to merge and the final close of the deal. The post-announcement phase is covered in more detail in Chapters 5 and 6. The timing and scope of due diligence varies from deal to deal.

In some cases, if both parties are interested, the candidate for acquisition will allow the potential acquirer a certain amount of access to its people, facilities, and data even before an offer is made. Often, the potential acquirer signs a nondisclosure statement stipulating that the information discovered will not be disclosed if the deal fails to go through. Sometimes agreements also prevent the potential buyer from competing for the candidate's customers. Many potential sellers have learned that opening their books and facilities to serious and qualified potential buyers can facilitate the process and indicate their own serious interest, provided that they are protected by a nondisclosure statement.

Affiliated Computer Services begins the initial due diligence by sending a two-page checklist of questions; it covers key areas such as the management structure, recurring revenue, major factors affecting profits, and any major lawsuits or customer problems the company is facing. Perhaps 50 percent of the companies they look at are eliminated on the basis of their answers to those questions.

When a company passes the initial screening test, ACS moves to the next stage, which involves asking the owners or the top managers more detailed questions. Chief Financial Officer and Executive Vice President Mark King of ACS says:

We tell our people, "Don't be afraid of stupid questions. Continue to ask follow-on questions; ask tons of questions. Don't just listen to their canned presentation. Ask 100 questions, 200 questions."

I have been involved in looking at between 1,000 and 1,500 companies over the years, and 80 percent of them say the same thing: They're expecting dramatic growth in the next couple of years, even if they haven't grown much in the past. They are going to get to tremendous synergies with ACS. They have an excellent, stable management team. They love each other. They've got this great, solid customer base. The new business they just signed is going to have a very high profit margin, the company is poised to explode, and so on.

They'll tell you that they just never focused on the sales effort—that's why they didn't grow in the past. They simply chose not to focus. And their expenses could have been brought down, but they chose not to focus on that either. You hear the same reasons from all these companies that they are going to do so much better in the future. You have to make sure that you're asking the questions that will get beyond those canned answers.[10]

Sometimes the senior management of the candidate company is either reluctant or legally prohibited from informing employees about the possible acquisition, but they are still willing to allow the potential acquirer some access. In these cases, members of the acquisition deal team may need to adopt pretenses for paying site visits. A check for environmental compliance, for example, might be presented as being done for insurance purposes; someone inspecting the plants might be introduced as a government inspector or a customer curious about manufacturing processes; an examination of the accounting records might be explained as an audit.

In other cases, particularly if the candidate is a competitor of the potential acquirer, no access is given. Legal restrictions may prevent leaders from giving a competitor too much information about the company's strengths and weaknesses, its proposed new products, and its future plans. It may be necessary to continue to rely on informed sources, publicly available data, and the information offered by the candidate's senior people.

These inputs generally lead to some preliminary conclusions about customers, pricing strategies, suppliers, cost and debt/equity structure, technologies, and health, safety, and environmental performance. Labor–management relations and the strength of union involvement, if any, can also be important, especially if staff reductions will be necessary after the acquisition.

The initial investigation is used to determine whether an offer should be made and to arrive at a preliminary valuation. Most companies that have an ongoing program of acquisitions have developed a formula for determining value. In the case of private companies for which little public information is available, knowledgeable people either inside or outside the acquirer's organization (e.g., investment bankers) are often able to come up with a valuation based on the price paid for similar companies.

Determining a price that is viewed as fair by both sides is a key factor in the post-deal success of an acquisition. In particular, if the buyer pays too much, it puts enormous pressure on the management team to show impressive results quickly after the close of the deal. This makes the already difficult task of integration even harder.

The Proposal: The Initial Offer and Letter of Intent

In a sense, the initial offer and, for acquisitions of privately held companies, the letter of intent are passports to the candidate's company: They ensure the kind of access that is needed to perform a more extensive, formal due diligence. The offer will be subject to conditions that can only be determined through a due diligence and should protect the potential acquirer if the due diligence reveals any surprises that mean the deal no longer looks viable.

Ideally, there should be no surprises: Experienced acquirers will tell you that they won't make an offer unless they have a very clear sense of what they will find when they go into the due diligence stage. As Senior Vice President of Business Development and Corporate Technology Don Knechtges of Geon (now PolyOne) says:

> We have never *not* done a deal based on surprises in the due diligence, and I think that has a lot to do with how we craft the agreement. You can protect anything with representations and warranties. And with privately held companies, we make sure the agreement puts the owners in a position where they are fully protected as long as they have revealed any problems. If there's anything we find out after the deal goes through, they will be heavily penalized. And if you find that the owners don't want

to sign that initial agreement, you know right away that something must be wrong. Let me tell you, that particular situation has engendered at times some very pointed conversation."[11]

There are a number of other legal provisions that may be introduced. Standstill provisions stipulate that the two parties involved will not acquire more than a certain percentage of each others' shares, preventing a hostile takeover during negotiations. Breakup fees that are payable if the deal fails to go through and other deal-protection devices are also common. Even though the process becomes very technical and legal at this point, Knechtges also had a surprising piece of advice for acquirers:

Never let lawyers negotiate these deals. We negotiate the deal and then instruct the lawyers to draw up the contract. You can never write down everything that can happen. So you need to have an agreement between the principals that allows those things to be handled when they are not covered by the agreement. If you have that kind of agreement between the principals, you can solve most issues that come up. And that's true with public as well as private companies: If the intent of the principals is honest, you can direct the lawyers to solve not only what was written in but what wasn't written in. Always trust the principals, not the document.[12]

Breaking Up Is Hard to Do: Walking Away from Deals

In the case of public companies, the approval of both boards of directors is required before the deal can be struck and the announcement made. Even if the CEOs of the company have agreed, their boards may not. The approval of compensation committees in each firm is also required if the senior executives' compensation packages are to be renegotiated.

But even when the boards are both in agreement, or if the company to be acquired is a private one where no such approval is necessary, the principals have to be prepared to walk away from the deal at any stage, from the first, tentative agreementto the final negotiations.

This seems simple enough, but it is natural for people on both sides to become emotionally involved in the acquisition, and breaking up is hard to do. Sometimes it is a matter of not wanting to see so much time and energy wasted. In other cases, leaders may be reluctant to admit that their judgment was flawed or may simply feel a certain attachment to the idea of the deal. At some point, people tend to start *wanting* the acquisition to happen and may resist facing up to the fact that maybe it shouldn't.

Glenn Goldman says, "The hardest thing is to remain objective. It's very easy to let the momentum of a deal and your emotional involvement get in the way of pulling the cord when you should. So, you react to things that should be major red flags by saying, 'We can overcome that issue.' But very often, it turns out that you can't. Sometimes the best thing you'll ever do is not to do the deal at all."[13]

Mark King of Affiliated Computer Services ascribes much of the success of the company's acquisition program to the fact that

> [b]ecause our acquisition group looks at over 150 deals a year but closes on only five or ten, they assume that more than 90 percent of them aren't going to happen. So they don't get emotionally attached. When the seller starts trying to increase the purchase price or starts making excuses for the problems that have surfaced, we just say, "Life's too short. We're onto the next deal." If we kill a deal on Monday, all that means is that on Tuesday one of the other acquisitions we're looking at becomes a higher priority. If people haven't worked on any other acquisition for years, they are going to find it much harder to walk away.[14]

Conducting a full due diligence is very costly in terms of time, effort, and financial resources. Some experienced acquirers have adopted a phased approach to the due diligence process: They focus first on the potential deal-breakers and then phase in work in other areas. This allows them to control their risk, minimize their initial investment, and walk away more easily if necessary.

The Engagement Party: Making the Announcement

In most acquisitions, the employees of both companies, the news media, the investment community, and customers are notified soon after the agreement is reached. As Senior Vice President of Corporate and Investor Affairs Dennis Cocco of PolyOne puts it:

We believe that our own employees should be told first, since they are shareholders; what we are doing is affecting their investment. Our CEO sends a letter to our employees, explaining the reasons for the proposed acquisition and describing exactly what is going on. Then we reach out to the employees of the other company; sometimes we do that through their own management, especially if the deal has not closed yet. We give their managers lots of information on Geon that they can disseminate to their employees as they see fit.[15]

AFFILIATED COMPUTER SERVICES' REASONS FOR ABORTED ACQUISITIONS RESULTING FROM DUE DILIGENCE

- Seller's profit projections were not realistic
- Monthly volatility in earnings results
- Management team was not compatible with buyer's management team
- Lack of contractual, recurring revenue
- Significant amount of earnings from nonrecurring sources (e.g., Y2K)
- Seller in industry segments that were perceived to be too risky by the buyer
- Poor geographic location (or location not desired by the buyer)
- Buyer determined that it didn't understand the seller's business—too risky
- Computer technology too outdated
- Restrictive software licenses
- Extended lease obligations offset potential synergies
- Significant future cash outlays were required
- Industry segment too regulated by the government
- Couldn't convince investor group that the purchase price was reasonable based on lower profit projections
- Disharmony among seller's management team

SOURCE: Affiliated Computer Services internal document.

Anything that can be done to get the truth into circulation early and check the proliferation of rumors is a good idea: As Mark Twain said, "A lie can travel halfway around the world while truth is putting on its shoes."[16] The anxiety and resentment that secretiveness engenders can linger for a long time and taint the integration process down the road.

In the case of the company that is being acquired, letting customers and suppliers know of the decision and its likely ramifications for them can also go a long way toward preserving their goodwill. When Charles Schwab, the discount brokerage firm, acquired USTrust, a provider of private banking services to individuals with high net worth, the bank's clients received a letter from the CEO via overnight mail, as well as a call from their bankers.

When it is handled well, senior managers on both sides of the deal spend the days following the announcement listening to employees and customers and communicating people's reactions and concerns back to the full leadership team. Typical concerns at this stage focus on benefits ("Will my insurance change?" "What about the 401K plan?") and possible reorganizations in areas that clearly overlap (when both organizations sell the same products to the same customer base).

The answers to many people's detailed questions are often not available at the time of announcement. In the absence of specific answers, effective leaders focus on explaining the rationale for the deal, helping people understand what each company does and what they stand for, and outlining how the integration process will be handled.

The Mating Dance

The mating dance that precedes the announcement of a deal is time-consuming and often emotionally charged. It needs to be conducted strategically, with the rationale for the proposed union firmly in mind. The further two firms and their leaders proceed in this process, the harder it is to back out. In addition, the tone and tenor of the relationship is established during this preliminary negotiation process, and this can affect the success of the merger "the morning after."

In the next two chapters, we'll deal with what usually happens the morning after the deal is announced and on the subsequent days until the close of the deal.

5

"WHAT HAVE I GOTTEN MYSELF INTO?"

Due Diligence and Pre-Close Integration Planning

If I were the CEO, I'd be gripped by cold, raw fear. Instead of drinking champagne, I'd brew a pot of black coffee.
—Consultant Stanley Hubbard[1]

The morning after the two companies have announced their intent to merge, the world is a different place. Commitments have been made; people's lives have been affected. Yet the decision is not irrevocable. A serious relationship has begun—but will the trip to the altar actually take place?

There is still time for cold feet, for second thoughts, or for interference by other suitors or outside authorities. After what may sometimes be a hasty proposal and acceptance, the two parties have a little time to step back and consider what they've gotten themselves into ("Was I crazy? Who is this person?"). That process is called due diligence.

In most cases, the due diligence process begins before the intent to merge is announced. Sometimes, however, very little due diligence is performed before the announcement. For one huge deal in the telecommunications industry, for example, an insider told us: "The CEOs got together, decided maybe they would like to get married, and came back and told everybody the wedding date. OK, they kind of eloped. There was very little due diligence that went into the original agreement. All of that was done after the fact."

Even in cases where substantial due diligence was conducted prior to the announcement, a great deal of work remains to be done to close the deal: regulatory approval (in some cases), legal matters, and the formal due diligence. It is at this stage that many companies fail to exploit opportunities for gathering information that can directly affect the success of the integration.

Getting Beyond the Numbers

Traditionally, due diligence has been the province of accountants and auditors, and certainly, careful review of the books of the company to be acquired is a mandatory and critical step in the process of merging. But after their first few deals, acquirers will tell you that the chief mistake they made during due diligence was to *limit* their data gathering to the obvious "hard stuff"—the financial data, the company's physical assets, its sales records, and customer information.

There are other kinds of assets, too, that the acquirer needs to familiarize itself with. It is these less tangible assets we will focus on in this chapter. If there are potential liabilities or expenses associated with these "softer" areas or if they will impede integration and therefore affect the success of the merger, these problems can and often do have direct financial consequences for the acquirer.

The Due Diligence Fieldwork

Fieldwork is what anthropologists engage in when they are studying a tribe or civilization closely: They take notes on the rituals, customs, kinship patterns, power structures, and artifacts of the group in question and then draw conclusions about its attitudes, beliefs, and values. We use the term here to refer to the work to be done when the acquirer has free access to the acquired company for the first time and can begin to explore its culture. When possible, members of the acquired company should be doing some of the same kind of exploration of the acquirer.

The Due Diligence Team

In assembling teams to conduct the due diligence fieldwork, it can be a good idea to go beyond the business development group and enlist the aid of as many corporate function staff people and line managers as is feasible. Not only will this mean more bodies to do the work, but it gets people involved in the integration from the start.

Obviously, specialized knowledge is required to evaluate information technology (IT) systems or manufacturing processes, both in terms of their overall adequacy and, as needed, their compatibility with the acquirer's systems. And it is vital for human resources people to be involved in HR due diligence, since they are the ones best equipped to ask the specific questions and anticipate the potential issues related to such critical areas as compensation, benefits, and HR policies.

The way a company structures these systems can reveal a lot about its philosophy and values. Offering generous leave for new parents or on-site child care, for example, says something about an organization's attitude toward work-family balance. People equipped to understand the implications of such provisions will be needed to make the assessment. Having HR people on the due diligence teams also serves as an acknowledgment of the importance of human resource issues in an acquisition.

In addition, as many line managers as possible should be involved, since these are the people who will ultimately be responsible for the ongoing, day-to-day integration, and they are likely to have a more finely developed sense of the acquisition's effect on customers and markets.

On the acquired company side, widespread involvement is also generally a good approach. Rather than collecting information only from those at the top, employees at all levels of the organization should be tapped when possible and given the opportunity to provide input. There are two crucial advantages to this approach: First, it allows for a much broader, deeper picture to emerge. Second, it can help to lessen fears and resistance by sending a clear message that people's input is valued.

Bruce Brodie of General American, which is now owned by MetLife, puts it this way: "The people who are closest to the war zone [people very involved in the integration work] are actually feeling the best. They have some feeling of control. It's really that next tier where there is a sense of 'You don't know who I am, and you haven't taken the time to appreciate who I am.'"[2]

Getting the Straight Scoop

There are a number of ways to gather information about a company once free access is possible. Interviewing selected employees one-on-one, though time consuming, can yield valuable insights. Conducting focus groups or surveys can also provide real insights. In addition, some companies conduct private investigations of key management people, to learn more about their track records and histories (a somewhat risky approach if it is discovered by the investigation targets).

But perhaps the most effective means of gathering the kind of information that's needed is informal discussions with employees. Mark King of Affiliated Computer Services has been involved in literally dozens of acquisitions both at ACS and at MTech, his former employer. He has the following advice:

> You ask a whole lot of questions, and you don't just talk to the top five people. Sometimes, it's a matter of getting there at 7:30 in the morning and seeing how many people are working then. Hang around the accounting group at 5:30 in the afternoon and see if there are still people there. I talk to accounts-receivable clerks. I ask them, "How is business going?" I am real friendly. I get people to talk, and I never act surprised by anything they say.[3]

King also emphasizes the importance of informal meetings between managers of the two companies—and not just for their value as get-acquainted gatherings.

> You invite the management team to your office so they can see how you operate. But you also invite them out to football games. You're trying to let them know you're not evil, you're just like them. So you go to the baseball games. You take them out drinking. In fact, some of the best due

diligence information that we have gotten has been over drinks, when people let their guard down. They say, "Boy, I'm surprised you would even be interested in buying us, since Customer C is about to go away." And you never let on that that's a surprise, but you might end up walking away from the deal, even after you've agreed on price and everything else, just because of what you learned from shooting the breeze with one of their managers over a few drinks.[4]

As another executive we talked to put it, "Companies are famously leaky, so always make sure you do more listening than talking during the due diligence process."[5] Sitting in as an observer at department meetings, unit meetings, and meetings of cross-functional teams assigned to specific projects can also be an excellent way of gathering data.

Whoever is involved and however the data is gathered, the more that can be learned about the two companies by both sides, the greater the likelihood of success of the integration. Beyond financial due diligence, experienced acquirers report great value in conducting:

- A cultural assessment
- A human resources systems assessment
- A health, safety, and environmental assessment
- An information technology assessment

Cultural Assessment and Planning for Integration

When two companies fail to merge successfully, the most frequently cited villain is "cultural incompatibility." This is undeniably true, but the phrase is so general and means so many different things to different people that it has become less than useful as an explanation for failure. Just as "irreconcilable differences" covers myriad marital problems, "cultural incompatibility" can be shorthand for many different difficulties in merging two organizations.

Organizational culture has been defined as "the shared attitudes, values, beliefs, and customs of a social unit or organization" or as "a set of assumptions ... meanings and values that form a kind of backdrop for action."[6] Culture can be seen in the actions of people in a company and in the underlying assumptions and values those actions express.

CULTURAL INCOMPATIBILITY

In 1996, the British Institute of Management surveyed executives involved in a number of acquisitions and concluded, "the major factor in merger failure was the underestimation of difficulties merging two cultures."

Examples of cultures that are strikingly disparate abound among … mergers and acquisitions.

Aetna Life and Casualty, which has been described as a stodgy, paternalistic, tradition-bound, sluggish organization that is slow to reach decisions, acquired U.S. Healthcare, described as a brash HMO, aggressive, scrappy, sophisticated, with an entrepreneurial spirit. Aetna's chairman, Richard L. Huber, called the marriage "messy"; after two years, the process is not over, having proved more difficult and costly than anyone anticipated.

The Price Club, whose employees have been described as having a "real-estate strip-mall mentality," merged with Costco Wholesale, whose employees have been described as "committed lifers" due to the fact that many rose through the ranks from being baggers. Although both firms are discount retailers, they couldn't work together and dissolved their marriage in less than a year.

SOURCE: Toby J. Tetenbaum, "Beating the Odds of Merger and Acquisition Failure: Seven Key Practices That Improve the Chance for Expected Integration and Synergies," Reprinted from *Organizational Dynamics* vol. 28, no. 2, Autumn 1999, p. 22 with permission from Elsevier Science.

While cultural compatibility certainly makes merging easier, differences in culture do not inevitably doom an acquisition. Compatibility need not mean sameness, any more than it does in a marriage. Perhaps what really need to be present are closely aligned values, which can be a different matter from behaviors, or "the way we do things around here."

Take customer focus, for example. One company's customer focus might take the form of delivering product on time, every time. The other's focus might take the form of working with customers to clarify and explore what they require and then figuring out how products and services can be modified or developed to satisfy those requirements. Because those two very different behaviors reflect the same underlying value, the companies could still be compatible, even though the cultures may be different.

Often the new, merged organization will require a different strategic emphasis; the culture that emerges may be slightly different from the previous cultures of either organization. Achieving that change successfully is more likely when there is a similarity of values.

While Cisco's due diligence team pays a great deal of attention to the culture of candidate companies, "It doesn't mean that we'll always walk away if it's not a perfect cultural match," says Mimi Gigoux. "You've got to weigh everything. I believe that there are a lot of cultural icons that are different from Cisco's that we can get beyond and still have a successful investment and a successful integration, but you have to be aware of them." Still, there are times when culture is a deal breaker, she reports: "I've had John Chambers [Cisco's CEO] say, 'I just think they're too different. I just don't think this is going to work.' Or I have said it, and the management team has taken my counsel."[7]

At Cisco, the evaluation of culture is the responsibility of every member of the due diligence team; HR is not the "culture cop," Gigoux says. "The engineers, when they go out for the second-level due diligence, are asking if they would like to work with these people. The management team will come back, and they'll be the first ones to bring it up: 'So, Mimi, did you notice the way So-and-So talked about his people?' Culture is a consideration in every single step of the process."[8]

A particularly ironic example of a corporate marriage that failed to address cultural differences was the much-touted merger of the Covey Leadership Center, headed by Steven Covey, the management guru and best-selling author of *Seven Habits of Highly Effective People*, and Franklin Quest. Having promised a "win-win deal with natural synergies,"[9] the two firms discovered too late that their organizations' cultures were very different, their products and markets had few overlaps, their philosophies of reward and compensation were foreign to each other—and no, their computer systems weren't compatible, either. Franklin Covey saw their salespeople leave in droves, their combined stock plummet by 54 percent in just eighteen months, their costs increase, their sales flatten out, and their earnings fall.

ASSESSING THE CULTURE

ACS is very good at sizing up the cultures of different companies. . . . they have this test tube thing they bring out and they pour
some water in it and have you drink it, and if it turns blue then you
know. No, actually they spent a ton of time with us before they did
the acquisition. They were with us through the whole letter of intent and due diligence process. It took well over a year for them to
do it, and we had several visits; we spent time. I spent time with
their president, Jeff Rich, even though it wasn't designed that I report to him. I got the chance to be with him and have him tell me
his philosophy one-on-one. They took the time to get to know us.
It wasn't just clairvoyance; they took time.

SOURCE: Interview with Group President Lynn Blodgett of Business
Process Solutions Group, ACS, and formerly head of Unibase Technologies, which ACS purchased in 1996 (purchasing the final 30 percent in
1998), December 1999.

Understanding the cultures of the two organizations starts with not-
ing the ways in which the underlying beliefs, values, and assumptions
manifest themselves—how the fundamental processes of running the
organization and conducting business are organized and handled.
While culture itself may be a fuzzy and hard-to-get-your-arms-around
phenomenon, it has some very specific and even measurable markers;
Bill Patient, retired chairman of the board of Geon, calls this "the
hard edge of culture."

People who are experienced in cultural due diligence and planning for
integration don't try to assess the culture directly; they don't ask a manager, for example, "So what's the culture like around here?" Instead,
they focus the data gathering on things like decisionmaking, organizational structure, communication, teamwork, employee satisfaction, and
readiness for change. When they understand how these pieces of the
puzzle work, they can assemble them into a more complete picture of
the culture.

Although we address each of these cultural elements separately later,
styles of decisionmaking, degrees of formality or informality, and the

THE BENEFITS OF OBSERVATION

People are always asking me "How do you keep from diluting Cisco's culture with all these acquisitions?" Acquisitions *are* Cisco's culture. A quarter of the population has come to Cisco through an acquisition. It's what we are.

I am on the deal team. Before the deal goes through, when we are having discussions about product vision and management systems within their company—frankly, it doesn't even matter what the topic is—we observe their decisionmaking. We observe where the enthusiasm comes from in the conversation, and if it's at the same place that we are feeling it, that's a sign that it's a good match. If it tends to be going in opposite directions from where we think the Internet and technology are going, then that's a sign that there could be a problem going forward.

But I also look at things like the mix of the people and their backgrounds sitting at the table. Sometimes it's what they don't talk about that seems most significant—the points that they don't bring up. Have they asked what the transition will mean to their people, or is it just what the transition will mean to the executive team? Is there a request to manage all of their own terms and close that out before they'll agree to the deal, but yet no reference to the overall population?

SOURCE: Interview with Human Resource Director of Acquisition Integration Mimi Gigoux of Cisco Systems, December 1999.

availability of information tend to be linked. In an organization in which senior executives hoard information, decisionmaking at lower levels will also be hindered. When decisions are made autonomously at the top, there is likely to be less teamwork (teams being essentially decisionmaking bodies) as well. Such a company will also probably have fewer two-way communication processes in place.

In addition to the possible incompatibilities in culture, an organization that operates in the ways described above will probably present more difficulties during the integration process. Employees who are accustomed to expressing opinions, generating ideas, making decisions, working in teams, and so forth will be more comfortable with the type of integration process described in this book, in which teamwork and input from people at all levels of the organization play a key role.

Decisionmaking

Who makes decisions in the organization? Is the CEO overly involved in day-to-day tactical decisions? How much decisionmaking power belongs to the heads of the business units versus corporate staff? To what extent do the people with the most direct contact with customers have the authority to make decisions?

The answer to "Who decides?" will also reveal something about the kinds of people who work there. Are they used to judging situations, deciding on the optimum alternative, and acting on their own initiative? Or is this a collection of people much more comfortable with following orders? And how does this employee profile fit with that of people in the acquiring company?

There is also the matter of decisionmaking *style*. Are decisions typically made autonomously by individuals or in consensus fashion by teams? Are other affected parties consulted during the decisionmaking process? Is complete consensus required in order to move forward, or does someone serve as the final arbiter?

Obviously, not all decisions within an organization are made the same way. There may be some group decisions, some in which the individual responsible for the decision first consults with others and then decides, some that are made unilaterally. Such a diversity of decisionmaking styles and procedures is wholly appropriate, given the different nature of different decisions.

But there is likely to be a distinctive mix in each organization. Ultimately, the best possible way to gather information on decisionmaking style is to watch managers in action. Interviews and questionnaires may also be used to flesh out the data, particularly if it isn't possible to do a lot of field observation in this area.

Organizational Structure and Hierarchy

The organizational structure of the candidate company is another piece of the culture puzzle. How many layers of management are there? Are people used to intensive, day-to-day, hands-on supervision? Or are they accustomed to taking action without waiting for management approval?

A factor that is often cited in accounts of failed mergers is incompatibility between a horizontal versus a vertical infrastructure. If a company with very few layers of management merges with a more "vertically" structured company with a complex chain of command, the potential incompatibility is significant and needs to be dealt with.

Differences in "style"—degrees of formality or informality, flexible hours versus rigid schedules—may be indicative of a deeper mismatch. Is the seller's culture casual and improvisational, or is it one with many detailed policies and procedures? How do people address one another? What are the dress codes? While these concerns may seem superficial, significant differences in the degree of formality can cause some of the most tenacious problems during the integration and beyond.

Again, probably the best way to get a sense of a company's organizational structure and the degree of formality or informality that prevails is to observe rather than to ask direct questions. Astute observers are alert for clues to the following:

- How people interact with their bosses and others at higher levels in meetings and one-on-one conversations
- How people in the staff units relate with people in line units
- People's freedom of access to others in the organization: Can they talk directly, or do they need to go through channels?
- The size of executive offices and other perks (one acquirer says she can tell a lot about the culture if the due diligence team is "shuffled off to the executive lunchroom" during discussions)

Communication

Companies vary greatly in the amount and degree of communication that is considered "normal": who knows what when, how open the conversations are, and how routine is it for information to be shared among levels of the organization.

Reviewing a company's formal written communications can be enlightening. What is the overall tone and level of professionalism?

What levels of effort and resources go into these materials? To what extent is technology leveraged as a communication tool?

How do they refer to the people who work in the company—as "employees," "non-exempts and exempts," "personnel," "associates," "team members," "cast members," or by using an even more unusual appellation? What kinds of job titles do people have? Are these titles truly reflective of the culture or just a clever idea?

And ask people specific questions such as: "How do you find out what's going on? Does your information come primarily from office gossip, your manager, your colleagues, formal announcements, e-mail messages, or another source? To what extent do you feel that you are well informed about the major initiatives and strategies of this company?"

Assessing the communication style of the organization also provides valuable information for the development of the integration communication plan—a critical element of the integration process.

Management Practices

Information on managers' behavior as coaches, consultants, communicators, inspirers, and influencers will be useful, not only to gain insight into the culture of the organization but also to start the process of evaluating overall management talent and identifying key and high-potential managers.

Asking questions about managers' styles and skills, as well as observing how these are viewed by their direct reports, will help to formulate a broad picture of the kinds of management practices in use. Particular attention should be paid to the behaviors required for success in the new organization. For example, if there will be more need to coach people in new areas of expertise or to build cross-functional teams, questions should focus on these behaviors.

In the interview or focus-group setting, it can also be useful to ask for anecdotes and for elaboration of responses where it seems appropriate. Sometimes, answers to follow-up questions provide the most insight.

Teamwork

Since the integration process will require a great deal of cross-company as well as cross-functional teamwork, it is also helpful to determine what sort of collaborative processes are now used in the organization. Questions such as these can be used during interviews to get a sense of the current level of teamwork:

- To what extent do others in the organization routinely share information with you and your team? Give an example of a time when information was shared or when it was withheld.
- How extensively do people collaborate across lines of business or functions? Have you been involved in any cross-organizational projects? Describe the experience.
- To what extent do teams in this organization have shared goals? How clear are team members about their roles and accountabilities?
- How is teamwork encouraged and rewarded here?

Employee Satisfaction

Understanding how people feel about working at an organization can provide very useful insight into what really goes on day-to-day. The level of employee satisfaction is also a basis for drawing conclusions about future performance and the probable degree of commitment to the merger effort.

Some specific questions to ask people in this area might include:

- Describe your work environment. (Take note of what is mentioned first or toward the beginning of the conversation and how it is described. This will be a key indicator of what is valued.)
- What do you value most about working at this company?
- What is the most difficult thing about working at this company?

Discrepancies between satisfaction levels and other information can sometimes be a warning sign that the acquirer should dig deeper. For example, if the data on human resources practices all sound good but employees don't have the enthusiasm about working at the candidate company that might be expected, it could be a clue to hidden problems.

Organizational Readiness for Change

A merger is the most dramatic change an organization and its employees are likely to undergo. An assessment of people's comfort with and readiness to change can yield important clues and are another piece of the culture puzzle.

To what degree are people encouraged to review and change the way things are currently done? How frequently do people experiment with new approaches or ideas to discover if they will be successful? In what ways does the reward system of the organization recognize and reward this kind of behavior?

What major changes has the organization undergone, and how were these changes managed? In particular, previous experience with integrating acquisitions can be quite telling. If these experiences were less than successful, what lessons were learned? What would they do differently next time? In our interviews for this book, many people cited prior experience with managing acquisitions as a key element in more successful later integrations.

Human Resource Systems Assessment

Another related aspect of due diligence and preliminary integration planning is to examine the policies, processes, and approach that the company uses to manage, motivate, and develop its people—its human resource systems.

Performance Management

A company's systems for goal setting, monitoring, and assessing people's performance can be a window into its culture. What kinds of behaviors and achievements are rewarded by the company's current systems? Entrepreneurial behaviors? Risk taking? Using a formal chain of command? Which is given top priority: People-management skills? Cost-cutting skills? Communications skills? Is the emphasis on evaluating financial performance, or are other things given significant weight?

How closely are the appraisal and reward systems aligned with the strategy the company is currently pursuing? Is there a direct correspondence between what the company says it wants from its people and what it measures them on and rewards them for? For example, does it claim to value teamwork across organizational boundaries but only reward managers on their own unit's financial performance? Such disconnects are common, and it's important to identify them so that these issues can be addressed in the design of the new organization.

Training and Development

What kinds of training and development experiences are being offered? What percentage of employees has attended training programs during the past two years? How easy or difficult is it for employees to gain access to outside training programs? Are they encouraged to seek out training and development opportunities? What skill areas are emphasized? Are they the skills that the company explicitly says are important to achieving its strategic goals?

In addition to training programs, the company may offer on-the-job development opportunities such as job rotation, mentoring, career path options, and support for individual career management. People are likely to expect the same degree of development support in the new company and be unhappy if it is not continued. In other cases, the acquirer may have more development resources to offer—an advantage that can be emphasized during initial communications to employees.

Compensation and Benefits

As might be imagined, compensation is "a big issue in any acquisition," as Robert Silver of PaineWebber puts it.[10] Are the two companies' compensation and benefit systems compatible? Often, there are significant discrepancies.

The *Wall Street Journal*[11] claimed that the compensation question was one of the trickiest cultural issues faced in the DaimlerChrysler merger. Chrysler executives received the high salaries that American boards of directors regard as fair for top people who are making their companies profitable. In most European countries, wide disparities between top executives' and workers' pay are frowned on. So whereas Chrysler's chairman was paid $11.5 million in 1997, Daimler's chief—the man he ultimately reported to—received $2 million. Obviously, the two different philosophies of compensation were bound to present problems.[12]

Even apart from the issue of straightforward parity, there is often a difference to be addressed in the way compensation is structured. For example, if the acquirer favors offering lower salaries and very high bonuses or commissions and the candidate does the opposite, the incompatibility obviously needs to be addressed in specific merger plans. Such a disparity can indicate broader philosophical differences, such as the degree of emphasis placed on individual initiative and entrepreneurship.

Compensation and benefits systems should also be analyzed with these questions in mind: First of all, do they provide incentives comparable to or better than the industry average? Are they adequate to attract talented employees? (This may provide a clue to the talent level of the organizations.) Second, are these obligations something the acquirer is prepared to meet? Are the pension plans adequately funded? Are there any potential harassment suits or other liabilities?

Labor-Employee Relations

The fieldwork in this area focuses on the extent, if any, of union activity; risk of Equal Opportunity Act suits or complaints; the tenor of employee relations at present and any possible negative impact related to the proposed merger; and any other legal issues of compliance that may be raised by the merger or by proposed staff reductions. Having an HR professional who is experienced with these potential issues conduct this part of due diligence is obviously desirable.

Health, Safety, and
the Environmental Assessment

Making sure that the company to be acquired is in compliance with all relevant health, safety, and environmental regulations is another key part of the nonfinancial due diligence and integration planning process. Obviously, the legal and regulatory risks to the acquirer if there are serious areas of noncompliance are high. And in cases where the acquirer's standards for health, safety, and the environment exceed the regulations, a less stringent approach to these matters on the part of the company being acquired can signal a difference in philosophy that could be problematic later on.

At a minimum, experienced acquirers say that they focus on the following points:

- The health of the workforce, as evidenced by the number of recordable and lost-time safety incidents, the amount of absenteeism, and any litigation that may have been brought against the company
- Compliance with health and safety regulations in all work areas, including use of proper equipment, inspection reports, and so on
- Compliance with environmental regulations, as evidenced by company policies on this matter, inspection reports, and any litigation that may have been brought
- The kind and amount of training offered to employees on health, safety, and environmental matters

Information also needs to be obtained about potential implications of plant or site shutdowns, in case these prove to be necessary. Some shutdowns may not be possible for environmental reasons. Or especially for sites located outside the United States, certain shutdowns may be forbidden by current government regulations or could be damaging to relations with the government of the country. Tax effects of possible shutdowns also need to be explored, so that decisions can be based on full information. In some cases, plant closings that occur prior to finalizing the deal or within a year of its going through can be written off as part of the cost of the deal. Such factors will need to be taken into account when the time comes to decide on this type of action.

Particular attention should be paid, experts agree, to environmental, health, and safety issues for potential acquisitions outside the United States, where health, safety, and environment standards tend to be lower.

Information Technology Assessment

Some of the most significant and costly post-close headaches can be avoided or minimized with a comprehensive due diligence and plan for information technology integration. Often, synergies and economies are anticipated, based on the forecasted ability to combine systems; frequently, these combinations prove either impossible or more trouble than they are worth.

When Union Pacific acquired Southern Pacific in 1996, rail cars were lost, depots were jammed, and ports were clogged. Shippers lost an estimated $2 billion in the fiasco, and in the end, the federal government stepped in to deal with the mess. Meanwhile, Union Pacific's dividend was cut in half, a result of the massive costs of their merger-related troubles. In the third quarter of 1997 alone, the added expenses and lost revenues occasioned by the merger cost the railroad $80 million.

Union Pacific had confidently predicted that it could gradually and smoothly convert Southern Pacific's outdated IT systems into synchronicity with their more sophisticated ones. But this plan called for the two companies to work together in tandem for a year while the systems remained different.

Incompatibilities in systems and in the ways the two railroads tracked their cars and trains proved insurmountable. For example, Union Pacific's main transportation-control system was built around car scheduling, whereas Southern Pacific's system was mostly an after-the-fact reporting system.[13]

In another instance, two companies involved in a merger assumed that their SAP enterprise-wide software systems would communicate easily with each other. Only once the merger was complete did they discover that the acquirer's system, which was the "large-scale" SAP product, and the acquired company's system, "ASAP" (the simpler, more basic version), were in fact totally out of sync. There was no way built into the systems for them to communicate. In the end, the acquired company's systems had to be scrapped entirely and a whole new system installed. The expenditure of time, money, and effort was enormous.

That's why conducting an IT due diligence and developing an IT integration plan are so important. Many of the problems Union Pacific faced, for example, could probably have been predicted if a careful analysis of the two railroads' systems and work processes had been performed before the acquisition went through. Whether Union Pacific's leaders had decided to proceed with the deal or not, they would at least have had a clear idea of where the obstacles would lie and could have started making plans to overcome them. Instead, each fresh disaster seemed to come as a surprise. According to Managing Partner Ronald N. Ashkenas at the consulting firm Robert H. Schaffer and Associates, "In almost every merger or acquisition we've studied, IT has emerged as one of the most critical aspects of integration. Yet about 90 percent of all acquisitions are done purely on a financial basis."[14]

Making an IT assessment as soon as possible can yield great benefits when the deal goes through. When Compaq Computer acquired Digital Equipment Corporation, the two companies managed to connect their networks "within hours," according to John White, CIO of Compaq. "That way we could send e-mail to everyone. There is a huge value in having your IT department provide a common infrastructure as soon as possible so everyone feels as though they work for the same company."[15]

In addition to assessing technology-supported communication tools, acquirers are wise to focus on the seller's IT capability to meet post-acquisition financial reporting requirements. This can be an issue when an acquisition involves the purchase of a smaller, privately held company by a public company with much more stringent reporting requirements.

Doing thorough IT fieldwork can also result in long-range advantages to the new, merged corporation. When the Bank of Boston (itself since acquired by Fleet) acquired BayBanks, Inc., for example, it adopted not only the smaller bank's retail strategies but also its IT systems for delivering innovative consumer products. "We at Bank of Boston were very focused on not destroying what we paid $2.2 billion for," said Michael R. Lezenski, Bank of Boston's chief technology officer.[16] With that in mind, Bank of Boston set about preserving the best features of BayBanks' IT systems, while updating some of their features and "cross-breeding" them with the acquirer's own systems.

"We took a look at what BayBanks did particularly well and what Bank of Boston did particularly well," says Bill Shea, vice chairman and CFO at the time of the integration. "If we weren't happy with what either place did, we tried to do something new and innovative."[17] Such an attitude pays off in terms of enhancing both morale and productivity and providing IT-based competitive advantage.

Drawing Conclusions: Core Competencies

When the above fieldwork has been completed, and ideally at several intermittent points along the way, the due diligence team assembles to share findings and draw conclusions. Apart from identifying potential risks, team members can also develop an assessment of core competencies—essentially what the company to be acquired excels at. These core competencies might be in areas like marketing, brand image, or product development or commercialization. Or they could be strong technological expertise, especially efficient manufacturing processes, the ability to tailor products to meet specialized needs, or an organization-wide customer focus—anything that sets the company apart from its competitors.

These core competencies need to be preserved and leveraged.

Assessing Potential Risks and Problems

It will also be time to draw some conclusions about the potential risks and problems associated with the proposed acquisition. These risks and problems should be articulated in the most specific terms possible, that is, not "potential IT incompatibility," but rather "the probability that their inventory systems cannot easily communicate with ours and expensive modifications or replacement will be necessary; downtime and customer dissatisfaction may result."

Or in the realm of culture, not "differences in management style," but rather "the likelihood that their customer service people will find it difficult to function effectively with fewer layers of management and may not feel comfortable making their own decisions about resolving customer complaints."

In the case of each potential problem identified, the following questions need to be posed and answered: Can we plan to avoid this problem or develop contingency plans to be used in the event it materializes? What steps can be taken to avoid it before it arises?

The process of planning to avoid each specific problem and determining how to deal with it if it occurs should be set in motion as soon as possible. Preliminary decisions need to be made about who will be responsible for making recommendations on how each problem or risk can be avoided or minimized. Should teams be set up for this purpose? And who should formulate the contingency plans to be put into effect if the worst scenario becomes reality?

Taking the Plunge: The Final Decision

At this stage of the proceedings, one or more risks or problems may be so serious as to make the acquisition undesirable. It is much better to acknowledge an insuperable obstacle and bow out gracefully even at this point than to plow ahead in order to save face and then wind up embroiled in a merger that never quite makes it.

Incompatibilities that are likely to lead to widespread revolt or even legal action should always be taken as serious warning signals. For example, compensation practices may be so different that the fundamental financial picture of the acquired company will be altered once its employees' compensation is brought into parity with the acquirer's. The purchase of a unionized company with significant labor relations problems by a nonunionized one may fall into the category of problems that cannot simply be labeled "to be worked out later." Other deal breakers at this stage have included the discovery of significant environmental or benefits liabilities.

Everyone involved in making the due diligence assessment needs to take the responsibility, when major issues surface, of bringing them to senior management's attention. Often, the momentum and enthusiasm for the project are such that people feel they can't possibly speak out against it at this stage. So doubts and suspicions are squashed, when perhaps they could have helped to avert disaster. It's important, therefore, for people to believe that their perceptions are welcome, whether positive or negative. It's better to call off the wedding even at this point than to proceed knowing in your heart that this is not the right move.

Most of the time, however, due diligence does not leave the acquiring company standing at the altar; more often than not, the deal goes through. When it does, the time-consuming and painstaking work of a complete due diligence provides solid reality-based information that is the foundation of the integration planning and implementation.

Pre-Close
Integration Planning

Many experienced acquirers actually begin the integration planning during the pre-close phase. Although there is always a chance that the deal won't go through, it's wisest to proceed under the assumption that it will. Therefore, while the due diligence is proceeding and before the deal is sealed, much planning work can and should be done. Legally, the two companies cannot actually begin to integrate, but they can certainly plan to do so.

A great deal can actually be done at this stage, much of which is covered in more detail in Part 2 of this book; this work includes:

- Identification of at least some and preferably all members of the senior management team
- Appointment of the integration manager(s)
- Identification of the integration teams and subteams
- Delineation of the external consulting resources needed for integration project management, communications rollout, and so on
- Clarification of the team launch process: team charters, deliverables, and communication tools and vehicles

Exploratory teams made up of key people from both companies can be established to begin to uncover possible synergies. One way to ensure that synergies related to both efficiencies and growth are considered is to create two separate teams, each focused on one kind of synergy. For example, one team might be charged with developing a preliminary list of synergies based on efficiencies to be gained based on the combination of the two organizations. The other would concentrate on identifying opportunities for growth and a broader scope of products and services that the new company can leverage.

Finally, at this post-announcement and pre-close stage, it can be useful to develop a set of guiding principles that will frame the integration effort. Examples of such guiding principles include:

- The goal of the integration process is to increase the value we provide to our customers.
- Business and functional experts from both companies will collaborate for optimal, balanced recommendations.
- We will attract and retain top industry talent by maintaining an industry-leading employee value proposition and creating fulfilling roles and career paths.
- The teams' work will be coordinated by the senior leadership team and the integration manager.

As you can see, there is still much work to be done. After the announcement and before the close, the true magnitude and scope of the integration task ahead begins to be felt throughout the organization. The challenge is to begin this work in ways that demonstrate the values and guiding principles that the new organization will stand for, while at the same time maintaining productivity and a focus on achieving the current goals.

Helping people focus on their current goals is probably the most important and most difficult task for leaders at this point in the process. Often, the value of the deal is contingent on the achievement of established short-term results and the stock price at the time of the close; therefore, it is critical that the organization stay focused on hitting the numbers that have been predicted. In addition, when people concentrate their energies and efforts on meeting these goals, they have less time or inclination to obsess about the uncertainty that the deal announcement always brings.

However much work is done up to this point, there is much more to be accomplished after the deal is sealed. Part 2 of this book describes the ongoing and challenging work of making the integration successful the morning after the deal closes and beyond.

Part Two

AFTER THE DEAL
IS SEALED

Several recent studies indicate that the lack of a coherent integration process lies behind the failure of many acquisitions. A Mercer Consulting study of companies generating post-acquisition returns to shareholders of $500 million or more found that the determining factor in an acquisition's success was neither the price premium nor the underlying strategy. Rather, success was most dependent on the way the integration was handled:[1] "For most companies, in short, the deal is won or lost after it is done."[2]

Fortunately, experience seems to be a good teacher. In fact, experienced acquirers—those that complete six or more deals per year–have a much higher success rate than less experienced ones, even when, as is often the case, the prices they pay are high.[3] What have those firms learned?

What are sometimes looked at—or scoffed at—as the "soft issues" related to integration are particularly important. In 1998 and 1999, Right Management Consultants undertook a survey of both acquirers and firms that had been acquired. Responses were received from executives in nearly 180 companies; each had experienced an acquisition within the past three years.

Among other things, the survey asked each respondent to rate his or her organization's effectiveness in dealing with the people issues related to the integration and how well it was performing on a number of objective indices:

- Reaching financial goals
- Improving market position
- Achieving strategic goals
- Garnering a better overall financial position
- Improving productivity and employee performance

The striking finding was that the companies that had handled the people-integration issues more effectively were also viewed as more successful in these critical performance measures.

Unfortunately, many acquirers don't recognize the need for comprehensive integration planning and paying attention to the human side of the equation. According to Myron Beard, a post-acquisition consultant with RHR International Company, "Post-acquisition is always the piece least attended to. Planning is the exception, not the rule."[4]

Gradually, however, leaders are recognizing that they need to attend to both the overall architecture and the details of the integration process if their firms are to avoid being added to the list of merger failures. But awareness of the need to plan for and manage the integration process is only the first step. It is much easier to understand conceptually what needs to be done than it is to actually pull off a successful integration of two companies. It's like the challenge of making a marriage work over the long term. We all know, for example, that effective communication is one of the keys to success; understanding that and actually communicating effectively are two different things.

One of the difficulties in managing the integration process lies in the overlapping, iterative, and complex nature of the work required early in the process. There are certain major categories of decisions and actions that need to be addressed, but it is not an entirely replicable process. In other words, there is work to be done, and it needs to be done well, but not in the same way or sequence every time.

Director of Business Development Peter Ruh, head of Cisco's Business Integration Unit, puts it this way: "There are parallel tracks. An integration is not one process—it's really a collection of many different processes. This is very much art versus science. You can't use a cookie-cutter approach; every deal is different because it's people, it's markets, it's emotion. We basically bring together all the right parties and then manage that every week for every acquisition."[5]

The major elements of the integration process, which as Ruh notes often run parallel rather than being sequential, are dealt with in detail in the rest of this book. These include:

- Staffing the senior team and clarifying the strategic direction
- Clarifying the integration strategy or architecture
- Managing the integration process
- Designing and staffing the new organization
- Communicating about the integration and new strategy
- Focusing on the ongoing development of the new company

6

CREATING THE FUTURE TOGETHER

Staffing the Senior Team and Clarifying the Strategic Direction

Wider participation in strategy-making means that senior managers, more than ever, must find a delicate balance between being decisive when required and encouraging others to make their own decisions.

—Stephen J. Wall and Shannon Rye Wall,
The New Strategists

The early stages of integration require strong and decisive leadership. People on both sides of the merger need to know who will be responsible for establishing their strategic direction and guiding them through the transition. There are a number of crucial decisions that remain essentially "on hold" until the senior management team is announced; the appointment of this team is one of the first and most critical steps in the merger process.

In some cases, the entire top team is announced before the deal closes. In others, the leader is announced first, with the rest of the senior management team appointed soon after. Sometimes, the top team is announced even later, after much of the transition work has begun. As you can imagine, this typically causes great confusion, and integration teams may have to redo many of their plans.

Staffing the Senior Team

Top staffing decisions send a very clear message to everyone in the new organization. In the inevitable climate of uncertainty and fear following an acquisition, the people selected for the top team will be scrutinized, and employees will work overtime to ferret out the true meaning of the team's composition. What proportion of senior-team members came from the acquiring company versus the acquired company? If the deal was announced as a merger of equals, as with the GTE–Bell Atlantic union, are there equal numbers of people from both sides? Most successful acquirers choose to include at least some members of the acquired company on the senior team; if this is not done, the difficulty of integration is greatly magnified.

And beyond the actual numbers, who was chosen for which positions? What do those decisions say about the kinds of people and values that will be emphasized and rewarded going forward? How will people within specific functions that will now be headed by executives from "the other camp" interpret the messages that are being sent?

The senior team announced in November 1999 for the GTE–Bell Atlantic (Verizon) merger included an equal number of executives from the two companies. Even so, people within the various functions had to deal with a "winner-loser" perception and the reality that the leader making the final call in their area might be from the other side. Although the integration teams for each function were also composed fifty-fifty of GTE and Bell Atlantic people with co-heads from each organization, issues that could not be resolved within the teams were escalated to the new head of the function.

In the human resources organization, for example, GTE's Marsha Cameron, co-chair of the HR integration team, reported, "There were a couple of incidences when one company or the other just has a really different philosophy about a certain type of benefit program or practice, and it's very difficult. You have to give it to a higher authority and have someone make a decision."[1] In this case, J. Randall MacDonald from GTE was appointed the Executive Vice President of Human Resources for the new company, and he was responsible for making the final call.

The composition of the top team is obviously a critical factor in the success of any integration. The skills and leadership styles of the senior people need to be a good match for the requirements of the new business. Clarifying the challenges that the business will face and the competencies that leaders will need to succeed is critical to making the best choices about who should be included on the leadership team.

Over the last fifteen years, we have developed and used a simple model that describes four overarching ways in which organizations respond strategically to their market environments.

When you boil it down, there are four general categories, or strategic states, that describe the thrust of the strategies that a business is pursuing. A business unit is following one of these courses:

- Creating a new business, product, market, or industry (an Eagle business)
- Maintaining or improving on a well-established current position in an existing market (a Fort business)
- Trimming product lines, production facilities, distribution systems, or markets served (Slim-Down)
- Fighting for the survival of the business (Circled Wagons)

Sometimes, of course, in a large business, all of these states are being pursued simultaneously at the portfolio level; leaders of specific business units, however, benefit from clarifying which state or grouping of strategies will be the key driver.

The strategic state of the new entity is an important consideration in staffing the top team. A start-up business or one in the process of creating a new product or market, which we call an Eagle, is looking for opportunities that have previously gone unnoticed. Like eagles, such companies attack without warning and choose prey that they can overwhelm swiftly. In other words, they avoid direct confrontation with massive market leaders. Eagle businesses are best staffed with people who can live with ambiguity and thrive on innovation and risk. Internet start-ups are Eagles, most of them fighting to become the first Fort businesses in an unproven and volatile marketplace.

An established and strong Fort business is focused on maintaining or improving its current position. While that may sound like a relatively staid strategy, when a Fort is a leader in its industry or is operating in a growing industry, this strategy is very dynamic. Success in a Fort organization requires a continuing pursuit of excellence, innovation and product or service improvement, increased differentiation from competitors, and constant attention to marketing. A Fort is always in danger of attack by competitors. Its ability to maintain or grow its market share depends on the ability of its people continuously to acquire and use new knowledge and skills.

As Eagles, such as America Online in the early days, become leaders in their markets, their senior teams need a different focus and skill set emphasizing efficiencies, standardized processes, and quality control. AOL's Steve Case may have realized this when he turned over the CEO reins to Time Warner's Jerry Levin. Case is the ultimate Eagle leader, and Levin's style is more like that of the general of a Fort. Even prior to the merger, AOL was making staffing decisions that recognized the need to fortify: Bob Glacel, who was hired in 1999 to run the operations of AOL's customer support call centers, is a former U.S. army general.

It's important to note that we're talking about the combined skills of the team here. The goal is to assemble a senior team with the constellation of experience, skills, and styles that are best suited for the strategic direction of the new entity; a business is not well served by a leadership team composed of people who are carbon copies of one another. Even the most entrepreneurial start-up business benefits from having some leaders who are inclined toward standardization and the establishment of replicable business processes. Likewise, a business that is focused on maintaining an already strong market share via proven, efficient methods can always use some innovative thinkers and new perspectives.[2]

Decisions about senior-team composition also need to take into account the degree of integration that is expected between the two businesses. In an alignment, for example, the senior team of the acquired company may remain more or less intact and separate, perhaps with a few more reporting requirements than before. A senior team managing a consolidation, on the other hand, is likely to be made up of more executives from the acquiring company, since the acquired business will be folded into the existing one. A synthesis works best with more equal representation from both sides.

WHAT IT'S LIKE TO
WORK IN AN ALIGNMENT

When I first heard we were going to be bought, I thought, "Right, I'm out of here." Because I've always needed a lot of freedom. I don't deal very well with bosses and structure and regular hours. I don't like meetings. That's why I was working for a small start-up company in the first place. And then we get bought up by the big guys, and I think, "No way am I going Corporate."

But it wasn't actually like that. It was okay. The paycheck had a different name on it, and the health-care provider changed, but there wasn't even any real difference in the two systems. And my work life went on pretty well the way it always had. I was talking to the same customers, working on the same kind of projects, trying to come up with new products. I had a couple of different people who were making inquiries about what I was up to, but they weren't meddling in any way. So one day I said to one of them, "You know, I really expected to leave when you guys took over. I didn't think I could take it. But it's not so bad. You leave us pretty much alone." And he kind of laughed, and he said, "That's why we did it this way. So we wouldn't lose all the mavericks like you that give this company its edge."

SOURCE: Interview with an employee of a high-tech company, July 1999.

Pre-Close Strategy
Development

The overarching strategy at the portfolio level is generally formulated before the deal is agreed to and closed. This high-level strategy work answers the following question: "Why are we adding this company to our mix of businesses?" Since at least some members of the senior team may not have been involved in these initial discussions, it's important for the new team to revisit the rationale for the acquisition and to reach consensus.

In addition, pre-close strategy work should also include the preliminary decision about the degree of integration expected. Where will this acquisition fall on the continuum of strategic organizing choices (alignment, synthesis, or consolidation)? These assumptions also need to be shared, discussed, and tested with the full senior team of the new business.

Determining the Business Strategies

Once the senior team is in place, the first question that its members need to wrestle with is this: "For what reason and how are we using this acquisition to differentiate ourselves in the marketplace?" Developing the business strategy for the new entity is one of their first responsibilities, ideally with substantial input from others. In many cases, this planning actually begins before the deal closes; if not, it certainly needs to be initiated very soon after. When the full senior team is not appointed until later, this strategy work is obviously made more difficult.

The goal of the strategic planning process is to develop a shared view of the market or competitive environment in which the new business will operate and what it will take to win in such a world. A shared view of this kind cannot be developed solely by senior managers reviewing planners' or consultants' analyses—it emerges only through discussion and debate among the leaders who will guide the business.

Deliberate strategic planning seems such a logical place to start that it's surprising how often this important step is omitted. After all, the strategic rationale for the deal was established earlier in the deal process, and senior managers may have been living with this rationale for some time before the deal is concluded. Therefore, they may overlook the following possibilities:

1. The management team may now include new people with different perspectives
2. Not everyone on the new management team may have the same understanding of the rationale for the deal

3. The reasons for the deal and the anticipated synergies are at this point only hypotheses that need to be tested and refined

Even in an alignment, when the acquired business will go on much as it has before, it's important for everyone on both sides to be on the same page strategically. This is particularly important when, as is often the case, the acquisition is a platform for similar acquisitions in the future. Leaders need to have a shared view of what the industry is all about, what the strategic goals are for both entities, and how these strategies support one another.

What Does the Industry Look Like the Morning After?

An acquisition creates a new configuration of assets, strengths, and weaknesses and a new market profile. Although the existing strategic plans for each previous business will certainly feed into the combined strategies, they will not fully reflect these new realities.

That said, the strategic business planning process that launches an integration effort is not significantly different from planning for any other kind of business. It first involves defining the industry and business—who you are and where you play.

A merger may throw a company into an established industry that is unfamiliar, as happened when GE acquired NBC. Or a merger may begin to define a new industry entirely, as the AOL–Time Warner combination is likely to do. How will that industry or group of industries be defined? Similarly, the deregulation of the utility industry in the United States is shifting the definition and the shape of this industry, essentially separating power generation from distribution.

Once the industry is defined, strategic planning requires examining the structural determinants of growth and profitability in that industry within an appropriate time frame. What is the anticipated growth rate of the industry? What do the competitive and customer mixes look like? What is the pace of technological change? How much government intervention can be expected?

When the acquired and acquiring companies are in the same established industry, such an analysis may be done fairly quickly, as a confirmation of existing assumptions. Still, differences in perceptions about what the industry is and what it takes to win can become readily apparent. Although Intercontinental Hotels and Holiday Inn, which were merged by their parent company, Bass, are both in the lodging industry, leaders from both sides soon realized that their views of the industry and the segments in which they compete were quite different.

When the acquisition combines companies from two different industries, a comparison can be particularly instructive. How are they similar? In what areas are they very different? Often the differences are most striking at the customer interface: Marketing driven versus sales driven; direct sales to end users versus distribution through middlemen; franchises versus company-owned distribution outlets. All of these factors make for significant differences among industries and industry segments, and it's important for the new senior team to spend time understanding those differences.

Where Do We Stand Now?

Within the defined industry, a competitive position analysis takes on particular significance in integration planning, especially where former competitors are involved. Here, the senior team examines marketplace profiles, comparing the new entity to its competitors.

What impact will the combined market share have on the industry? Will it provide an opportunity for pricing leadership—can the business raise prices and will competitors follow the lead? Exxon and Mobil may each have had a fair amount of pricing power, but the merger created an even bigger giant that will vie for industry leadership with Royal Dutch–Shell and the new BP Amoco–ARCO combination.

And how has the acquisition affected the product line/service breadth of the new company? If global reach was the goal, as it is with many of the telecom mergers in Europe, what will that do to the smaller, one-country companies? If the merger significantly changes the market profile relative to competitors, what reactions can be expected and planned for?

What is the brand reputation or image associated with each business? What does this imply for the entity going forward? While Chemical Bank clearly acquired Chase, for example, Chemical took the Chase name, banking on the better-known brand. Commissioning market research by an objective third party can be particularly useful, since the internal perceptions of a brand may not be the same as customers' views of it. Research can also help to resolve differences of opinion on the team about the respective brands of each business.

What special customer relationships have been developed, and how will the merger affect these relationships? Key customers need to be considered on a case-by-case basis. Did they deal with both companies before the merger? On what terms? How can these relationships be maintained and leveraged?

You can see that even though those on the senior team are focused on high-level strategic analysis at this point, they also, out of necessity, are dealing with very specific short-term tactics. In an integration, there are a number of short-term issues that need to be addressed immediately, and dealing with key customers is at the top of this list.

Other longer-term questions to be covered in the competitive analysis include: What is the potential impact of the merger on the business's cost position? Can economies of scale be predicted, and if so, how will they be realized? Is the combined might of the two companies likely to make for greater leverage with suppliers, and which side has the stronger supplier relationships?

Overall, what does this merger add to the ability of the new entity to compete and add value in the marketplace? And what does the leadership team need to do to capture that value and those synergies?

These questions should obviously be considered prior to deciding to do the deal in the first place. Even if a careful competitive analysis is done before the deal is closed, however, it's important to revisit key assumptions and conclusions with the full new management team.

What's Next?

The industry and competitive analyses are in essence a snapshot of the new landscape that has been created by the combination of the two firms. This work is necessary, but certainly not sufficient. The question "What's next?" remains to be answered.

Given the new marketplace configuration, what should the strategic direction of the business be? What is our vision of this business for the future? These are the tough issues facing the senior team and the organization as a whole. And coming up with shared, compelling answers to them is key to driving the integration forward, to uniting the two organizations with a common goal and set of strategies.

Anticipating and preparing for a variety of scenarios is a key and often overlooked part of the strategy process. As with due diligence, many people don't really want to explore the downside scenarios as thoroughly as the upside ones. As one research report for the utilities industry put it, "There seems to be greater enthusiasm for the upside potential than the downside risks of new business opportunities. Everyone expects to be a winner."[3]

Even when all this strategic analysis has been done, and done well, the most effective leaders know that any strategy is really just a best guess about what it will take to succeed. The plans and direction will still need to be tested in the marketplace and shaped over time.

Strategy and Degrees of Integration

Thoughtful and reality-based strategic analysis forms the basis for decisions about the optimal degree of integration. These decisions are usually iterative, not sequential. In this book, we had to make a choice and put something first, but in actuality, the best strategy and most appropriate degree of integration tend to emerge more simultaneously.

When Ford acquired Jaguar, for example, executives recognized that each side had developed some competitive advantages that needed to be preserved. Jaguar had a strong brand cachet based on its styling and history, and it brought to Ford the luxury car that had always eluded the American automaker. However, the Jaguar reputation for quality was dismal; the saying went that you needed two Jaguars—one to drive while the other was at the garage. Ford brought strong quality processes and massive resources to the deal. The strategy was to shore up Jaguar's quality, while at the same time capitalizing on its strengths.

This strategic rationale led to a decision to synthesize the two businesses, taking the best of both. The strategy drove the decisions about how to integrate the two companies, and over the longer term, the integration design helped to shape the strategy as it unfolded.

Strategy and Vision

Significant shifts in strategy after an acquisition or a series of them can require the development of a new, shared vision for the new entity. This, too, needs to be driven by the senior team.

At Geon (now PolyOne), for example, a number of acquisitions over the past several years have, by design, changed the focus and the face of the company. In 1999, the senior team, led by CEO Tom Walter-mire, realized that these changes necessitated revising the Geon vision. With significant input from people at all levels in both the original Geon organization and the companies that had been acquired, the vision was revised, although the company's formal "Guiding Principles," or statement of values, remained constant.

The new vision was developed to help people align their work with the new strategic direction of the company. Once basically a commodity-driven manufacturer of polyvinyl chloride (PVC) resins, Geon was transforming itself, both through acquisition and divestiture, into a global provider of performance polymer solutions. The new vision reflected those changes: Geon would be more global, offer a wider range of polymers to meet customers' needs, and emphasize value-added services, such as resin compounding.

One of the elements that was revised was the title of the vision, which had previously been "The Geon Way." Based on feedback from people in acquired companies, who felt that this implied "our way or the highway," the title was changed to "The Geon Commitment."

The new vision was communicated to the entire company in 2000; the rollout process and materials were customized to meet the unique needs of various acquired businesses. Geon used a series of interactive meetings led by the managers of the businesses and functions to reach every member of the organization and help them understand the rationale for the new vision and what it meant for their day-to-day work.

Underscoring the ongoing nature of this vision development and communication work, Geon announced its merger with M. A. Hanna, a competitor twice its size, in May 2000; this vision development and rollout process will begin again, reflecting the views and goals of the new, much larger entity: PolyOne.

THE GEON COMMITMENT AND GUIDING PRINCIPLES
JANUARY, 2000

The Geon Commitment

A valued partner.
A trusted neighbor.
A sound investment.
A winning team.

Geon is a growing, global provider of performance polymer products and services. Our closely aligned network of businesses is **committed to creating real value** for Geon's customers, communities, shareholders, and people.

Our customers value us as a distinctive and strategic resource. Our innovative technologies and solutions make them leaders in their markets.

Geon is the leader in health, safety, and environmental performance. **Our communities** are better because we are there.

We earn the leading market position in each of our businesses. We produce superior, predictable returns for **our shareholders**.

Our people are the highest-performing team in the industry. Personal growth and continuous improvement drive our success. We aggressively seek new ideas and share our knowledge across the company.

Guiding Principles

Respect for the Individual

Openness and trust permits us to face all challenges honestly and is grounded in our basic respect for the individual.

The total **involvement and contribution** from every individual is what makes us special.

Empowerment means that we each take the initiative to solve problems and achieve our vision.

Learning and development fuel the personal and professional development vital to long-term competitiveness.

(continues)

(continued)

A lively **diversity** of ideas and backgrounds gives us the creativity to succeed in a rapidly changing world.

Excellence

We bring a **clear purpose and mission** to every activity.

We take **great pride** in our achievements and at being the best at whatever we do.

Continuous improvement of our work processes and products is everyone's personal responsibility. We have the courage to try new ideas and learn from failure.

We are committed to providing superior **service to customers and each other**.

Teamwork multiplies our individual and functional efforts into successes for Geon as a whole.

We share our knowledge extensively for the betterment of the business.

Integrity

Our commitment to **excellence in safety and environmental performance** is absolute.

Geon's sense of **community and responsibility** makes us "good neighbors" in every sense.

Ethical behavior and compliance with the law, both in spirit and in letter, guide every activity.

Involving Leaders at All Levels

Our emphasis has been on the role and responsibilities of the senior team in the planning process, and they really do need to drive the effort. It cannot be delegated to even very competent strategic planning, human resources, or communication staffs, or to temporary integration teams. The senior managers of the new entity must own the vision and strategies and be fully committed to communicating and implementing them.

That said, our bias is to involve people at all levels in strategy making as much as is feasible.[4] This can be particularly challenging in an integration situation, when there is a strong sense of urgency about

A NEW APPROACH TO STRATEGY

Businesses today are facing a broad array of new challenges, and those challenges require a new approach. They are turning to wider participation in strategy-making to help them achieve an advantage over their competitors in a rapidly changing market arena. This input is paying off, according to a research study conducted by Gordon Group, Inc.... This study found that "companies that involve employees more in decision-making boast stronger market valuations than those that don't."[5]

SOURCE: Stephen J. Wall and Shannon Rye Wall, *The New Strategists: Creating Leaders at All Levels* (New York: Free Press, 1995), p. 22.

arriving at strategic decisions. After all, very little else in the integration effort can move forward until the overall direction and structure are established.

Compared to other nonmerger situations, the senior team may very well need to move ahead with less input than would otherwise be optimal. This situation is somewhat mitigated if both merging organizations have a history of wider involvement in strategy making; their pre-merger plans already reflect the input of people outside the senior management ranks. When this is not the case, however, the senior team must perform a skillful balancing act, making important decisions with appropriate speed and with adequate input.

This need for input certainly does not imply taking a companywide vote as to the wisdom of a suggested strategic direction. It does, however, mean taking a bit of extra time to get the ideas and suggestions of key managers and people whose support will be required to implement the changes that are coming down the pike. It may mean conducting a few focus groups composed of people at all levels—as one of our clients did recently—before announcing a new vision to determine whether it is seen as relevant and inspiring. (In this case it wasn't, and they went back to the drawing board.)

Challenges in Strategic
Planning for Integrated Businesses

In addition to the challenge of getting wider involvement under tight time pressures, the senior team faces a number of other challenges during the initial planning process.

If the team is composed of people from both the acquired and acquiring businesses, this is a time when all kinds of differences can come to the fore. Cultural differences—particularly related to decisionmaking speed and styles, the degree of formality, and the importance of hierarchy—are likely to emerge fairly quickly. No matter how complete the cultural due diligence was and how good a fit the two companies seem to be, there will always be some differences in their styles and approaches.

As frequent observers of meetings in a wide variety of companies, we can vouch for the fact that every organization's norms and culture are unique. In some companies, blunt, frank exchanges and aggressive debate are common; others are characterized by more polite exchanges (sometimes followed by behind-the-scenes maneuvering). Formal presentations are a way of life in some firms; others emphasize informal discussions and one-on-one meetings.

Even very basic issues such as the normal mode of distributing information (e-mail, voice mail, and so on) can become distracting bones of contention. One manager in a recently acquired company told us that what disturbed him most about the people in the new owner company was that "[t]hey just announce that I have to be at a meeting on a certain date without ever checking my availability, and they never, never say thank you."[6]

The normal speed of decisionmaking can be another key culture-based difference. In the case of MetLife's acquisition of General American, the acquired company's management team actually pressed for the immediate sale of the group health insurance business. According to Bruce Brodie, CIO of General American, "Met was pretty content to make that decision later. Our business people said, 'You need to sell us. The market's going to know that you don't want us long term, and we will be dead in the marketplace. You'll kill us.'"[7]

Even the strategic planning process itself may prove to be a bone of contention, if senior managers are wedded to their customary way of doing things. As should be clear at this point, all of these issues cannot be resolved, nor can all of the initial planning work be done, at a one-day meeting.

Significant investment of time and thought is required to arrive at the optimal strategic direction for the new entity—and the work has only just begun.

7

FORM FOLLOWS FUNCTION

Arriving at the Integration Strategy

> *Form ever follows function.*
>
> **—Louis Henry Sullivan, "The Tall Office Building Artistically Considered,"** *Lippincott's Magazine*, **March 1896**

The strategic direction of the new entity serves as the framework for the entire integration effort. Yet leaders of many acquiring organizations fail to realize that there is more than one way to integrate and that the integration strategy needs to reflect the overall business strategy for the new entity.

Arriving at the best decision about the integration strategy means coming to agreement on the optimal degree of integration of the two organizations. Having a common framework and vocabulary can be very useful; our integration strategy model (Figure 7.1) offers just such a framework.

While the degree to which two organizations can integrate falls on a continuum, we have identified three basic integration strategies, with

FIGURE 7.1   Determining the Integration Strategy

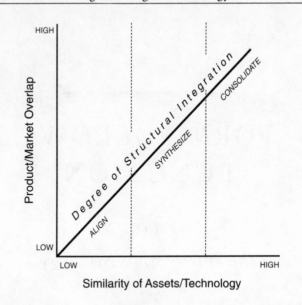

consolidation on one end, alignment on the other, and synthesis falling
in between. Each is appropriate in specific merger situations, and each
brings its own challenges related to managing people issues in particular. Let's look in more detail at each integration strategy in turn.

Consolidation:
The Corporate Bear Hug

In a consolidation, the acquired company is essentially folded into the
acquired company in a big corporate "bear hug." In most cases, it simply does not continue to exist, and most of the acquirer's policies, procedures, and cultural characteristics are adopted.

The most commonly cited reasons for a consolidation are the need
to achieve economies of scale and the desire to gain market share.
These reasons are often mentioned in the same breath and are assumed to coincide.

In their attempt to do more of what they have done in the past and do it more efficiently, many companies are buying up others that provide the same services or products and consolidating them, absorbing those companies into their own. That generally means fully integrating the infrastructures of the two organizations, creating a single, unified customer base.

The reasoning behind this type of integration is that the consolidated organization will achieve greater economies of scale and thereby greater earnings growth. It will, in theory, become more efficient, delivering the same amount of goods or services with fewer assets or more goods or services with the same assets (while growing over time at better than market rates).

In turn, this will allow the organization to either fatten its margins and be more profitable or lower its prices while maintaining margins that are superior to competitors' and gain market share. Either choice seems a logical route to greater profitability. Why, then, do anticipated economies of scale so often fail to materialize?

Economies of Scale

For one thing, the efficiencies to be gained from economies of scale (certainly in terms of manufacturing and distribution economies) are curvilinear. At some point, there is a limit to how much more efficient an organization can become. As competition heated up and the Quality movement took hold, many companies became extremely efficient in the 1970s, 1980s and 1990s. There isn't always a lot more efficiency to be wrung out of the system.

Nor are economies of scale automatically achieved just by becoming bigger and acquiring market share. Achieving real economies of scale requires streamlining business processes, consolidating physical assets, rationalizing the product mix, leveraging buying power, optimizing the supply chain, and ensuring that people are managed in such a way that their personal performance and productivity are maximized. Too often, acquisitions fail to reach their potential because this very real and difficult work is never done.

Finally, economies of scale on their own may no longer be a sufficient goal strategically. Michael Porter's traditional view of competitive strategy contends that businesses face a clear-cut choice. They can compete either by being low-cost producers or by creating products that are differentiated from those of competitors. If cost is the chosen basis of competition, economies of scale are key.

In the real world today, however, few businesses have the luxury of being able to choose low cost as the only basis of competition. More and more, businesses need to be low cost *and* attend to the unique needs of special market segments. Being able to customize on a mass basis is becoming possible and, in some cases, a competitive necessity.

Porter's dichotomy has been made less relevant because information about customers, markets, competitors, and suppliers is available in real time; it is also possible to exchange information directly with all those links in the chain.

Much attention has been paid to the ways in which enterprise resource planning (ERP, or "wall-to-wall") systems are changing the way we work by giving people inside the company access to all the information they need for better decisionmaking. But what may be even more significant is the advantage that electronic, on-line information and the existence of e-commerce can and will provide in business-to-business relationships. More exact knowledge of both customers' needs and suppliers' market conditions enables companies to find new, more efficient ways of producing what is required to meet the specific demands of the market. (That's why Cisco has totally revamped its enterprise-wide resource planning systems not once but three times in the past six years—so that every employee, customer, and supplier can have instant access to all the data they need.)

Another reason that the price versus differentiation dichotomy no longer applies is that we now have a much clearer understanding of how to manage business processes. Business-process improvement allows for both greater efficiencies and greater tailoring of products to markets. Processes become more efficient as the number of transactions is reduced. Efficient processing of information between a business and its customers allows for more timely and complete understanding of market needs.

In summary, economies of scale are more difficult to achieve than is often recognized. And even if leaders manage to gain such economies, the advantages they bring will not be the Holy Grail they were once assumed to be.

BMW, for example, is betting that a midsized automaker can survive and thrive amid its much larger competitors. Joachim Milberg, the CEO, has led the development of "one of the two most brilliant manufacturing systems in the entire industry."[1] The company's flexible factories, which can quickly switch to producing the models most in demand, are "way ahead of those of most of its rivals in delivering the nuts and bolts of this revolution,"[2] according to the *Economist*.

However, there are still certain advantages that go hand in hand with size, and these may be adequate justification for taking the consolidation approach to integration. Global reach, more negotiating and purchasing power, access to capital, and even more power over customers in highly consolidated industries—these can all provide a real edge. But none of it happens automatically; reaping the benefits of size requires careful management and the full contributions and commitment of people at all levels.

When Does Consolidation Make Sense?

Essentially, consolidation is appropriate when the organizational units being integrated provide very similar functions or when the acquired company provides the same products and services to the same markets as the acquirer. When PaineWebber, for example, acquired Kidder Peabody, the two companies' products, services, and markets were virtually identical, which meant that a high degree of consolidation across all functions was appropriate. Still, some unique features of Kidder's products and the processes that supported them were preserved, and PaineWebber largely avoided the "arrogant acquirer" mistake, adopting some of Kidder's processes and practices.

Most acquisitions require some consolidation in some area of the business. The protean organization, in its process of adapting to its environment, may consolidate and perhaps "deconsolidate" on an ongoing basis.

As noted earlier, Time Warner (before its own acquisition by AOL) achieved a nice balance between consolidation and alignment by consolidating back-office functions and leaving entities like *Time* magazine alone. It's an approach that is becoming pervasive in the publishing industry. Similarly, in the 1996 merger of composites manufacturers

THOUGHTS ON CONSOLIDATION

If you're acquiring someone doing the same thing you're doing, you don't have to spend a whole lot of time figuring out just what they do for a living. Our main focus in buying Kidder Peabody was on growing our core businesses. We were very clear on wanting to grow the core businesses, not go into different channels.

You always need to ask yourselves, "Will the marketplace respect this acquisition—will it be perceived as additive from a public relations standpoint?" Say the other firm has had bad publicity about its sales practices or its products: You have to decide if you can get over that.

You also need to ask yourselves, how sticky is the business? PaineWebber's business is very portable—our clients are tied to the producer, not the firm. If you buy a firm that is the same, and the producer leaves, you are buying a bag of air.

SOURCE: May 1998 interview with Executive Vice President of Operations, Systems, and Services Robert Silver of PaineWebber, reflecting on PaineWebber's acquisition of Kidder Peabody in 1993.

Hexcel and Ciba (part of Ciba-Geigy, Ltd.), certain plants and marketing units were consolidated, while other plants and functions that were related to specific customer groups or specific capabilities were left to operate as they had before the merger.

The question that needs to be asked is: "What areas or functions can be consolidated for greater efficiency *without* destroying a possible basis for competitive advantage?" That is, can consolidation be accomplished while still providing an equivalent product and serving the market as well as or even better than before? Can consolidation be done in a way that does not adversely affect customers' perception of the value they are accustomed to getting?

Lack of attention to this issue is another common failure factor for acquisitions. Sometimes, a feature that the acquirer sees as irrelevant to competitive advantage might seem absolutely crucial to the customer; what looks to the organization like an equivalent product just isn't as good in the customer's eyes. Thus, what the organization regards as making a minor change can have a major impact on sales, as we saw with Novell and WordPerfect.

In the rush to generate quick wins based on consolidation, some very bad decisions can be made. When First Union bank acquired CoreStates in November 1997, First Union, like many of the big financial institutions, was counting on big cost reductions based on consolidation. Branches were closed; people were laid off; service deteriorated. First Union saw 19 percent of CoreStates' customers defect in an eight-month period and even rehired some employees to improve service.[3]

People Issues in a Consolidation

While staffing issues are important elements of any acquisition, they are particularly central in a consolidation, which generally calls for a certain number of layoffs: The likelihood of duplication of staff in a consolidation is obviously much higher than in other types of integration structures.

Although the logical decisions related to eliminating redundancies are often quite obvious, the emotional toll on senior managers can be greater than in a synthesis or alignment. One executive told us, "The acquirer also experiences stress. One of my kids turned against me because I had to shut down a plant in our town. His friends were affected, because their parents were going to lose their jobs. They saw me as the guy who was taking the jobs away from their parents. For us, it was a roller coaster on a number of levels—personal, emotional—it can even trigger some physical symptoms."[4]

Because losing a job or the fear of losing a job is the most sensitive issue—the "me issue"—in an acquisition, it is also the issue about which clear, open, ongoing communication is absolutely vital. Speaking of the Glaxo-Wellcome merger in 1995, Director of Organizational Effectiveness Steve Sons of Glaxo Wellcome, formerly of Glaxo, says,

> We told employees what we could as quickly as we could, including what all the severance packages were, right up front. We couldn't tell people whether or not they had a job, but we told them what would happen to

them if they lost their job very shortly after the merger was made. We had town halls and we had videos, we had worldwide publications on the merger, we had local and regional publications. We really flooded people with communications.[5]

Even with the best and most open communications, a consolidation will be difficult for people to deal with emotionally. Johanne Paquet Belzile, a chemical engineer and the wife of an executive who has led a number of integrations, reminds us eloquently of the difficulty:

> People will not renew magazine subscriptions; they won't buy new furniture, get tickets to a show, or make decisions about their kids' college until they know what's going on. Some people may eventually become very rich from the merger and be very happy, but for the majority of people, what is created is a very insecure environment. The longer it takes to tell people what they can expect and what is going to happen, the more miserable you are making them.[6]

While we are generally opposed to making integration decisions speedily for speed's sake, in the case of consolidation and layoffs we do think faster is generally better—*as long as the strategic rationale for them is sound and the potential impact on customer value perceptions has been thoroughly considered.*

Companies that have to engage in large-scale staff reductions must deal with the problem of lowered morale, and therefore less than stellar performance, among departing employees. Some companies handle this issue by offering not only outplacement counseling but also substantial termination bonuses for any employee who maintains high performance levels up until the time of leaving.

This not only provides departing employees with an incentive to continue to perform at high levels but also helps to shore up morale among employees who are staying on. It sends a clear signal that the acquiring company has a sense of responsibility toward the employees of the company it has acquired and reassures those remaining that they, too, will be treated fairly and decently. The sensitivity with which this issue is handled can have a major impact on the company's ability to retain the people who have been identified as crucial to the organization's future.

Alignment: Enhancing the Portfolio

Alignment is at the other end of the integration spectrum. A straightforward alignment, which can take the form of a wholly or partly owned subsidiary, allows the acquired company to continue to operate as a separate entity within its own market environment, often with its own mission, structure, systems, staff, and culture.

There are many cases of acquisitions where all that is needed is to align financial reporting. That's the approach Affiliated Computer Services has taken with many of its acquisitions. It has left them to operate as they did before, only "under the ACS umbrella," to use the phrase employed by Lynn Blodgett, who sold his company, Unibase Technologies, to ACS and then stayed on to manage it.[7]

In some ways, an alignment resembles a partnership arrangement, though the power equation is different. But like a partnership, it can be structured to allow for sharing of customer information and intellectual capital or co-development of products and services, even while the two companies remain relatively separate.

Twenty or thirty years ago, there were two main assumptions underlying such an acquisition. One was that the acquirer had management talent at its command that was unavailable to the company being acquired and could add value to that company almost as a matter of course. The ability to manage a company effectively in what was becoming an increasingly complex business environment was in short supply. Long-range strategic planning and employee development efforts were carried out in relatively few companies then; professional business and financial management was the province of specialists. That situation has changed radically.

The other assumption that made alignment through acquisition seem like a good idea thirty years ago was that it provided the acquired business access to capital that it would have had more difficulty obtaining otherwise. Leaders of smaller companies who wanted to expand rapidly had limited access to the capital they needed to do so; only the larger corporations could command the kind of financial resources necessary to help a company grow. The situation today is very different; our capital markets operate with extreme efficiency.

When Does an
Alignment Make Sense?

But what is the point of an alignment now? What is its justification in the twenty-first century? While the acquired company may still hope to get access to financial and other resources that it could not muster on its own, the acquirer is likely to talk about the purchase in terms of diversification of its portfolio, thereby reducing risk. That is, it hopes to decrease the variability of its cash flow; it prevents the company from having all its eggs in one basket.

Does such an acquisition and such an approach to integration often achieve the desired result? Does diversifying a corporation, like diversifying a stock portfolio, really reduce vulnerability by providing a safeguard against the vagaries of the marketplace?

Our answer, in many cases, would be a qualified "no." Part of the problem can lie in the very difference between what the acquiring and acquired firms do for a living. Paradoxically, when a company diversifies in order to reduce its risk, it may also increase its risk. The risk here is that it cannot always make good decisions about, first, evaluating candidates for acquisition and, second, managing the acquired firm or helping it to grow once the merger has taken place.

Acquisitions meant to achieve diversification are more likely than same-business acquisitions to be evaluated in purely financial terms. The acquirer won't have the kind of long-standing familiarity with the other company's business, markets, customers, and employees that would enable it to evaluate the acquisition as a whole, rather than as an array of numbers.

This problem can persist after the acquisition, when financial performance alone is often the only way for the leaders of the parent company to judge the capabilities of the aligned entity. Thus, they may fail to recognize when poor performance has to do with factors outside the business's control, as is often the case in a highly cyclical industry. They may not make good management decisions or good strategic decisions because they do not understand the critical determinants of success in the acquired business.

In fact, this may be one reason that acquirers have often wound up with acquired companies worth much less than they paid for them, as was the case with Ralston Purina's purchase of Eveready Batteries. At the time, Eveready was a leader in its market. However, Ralston forced Eveready to emphasize marketing targets focused on buyers at supermarket chains and took drug, hardware, and sundry stores for granted. The result has been that competitor Duracell has gradually emerged as the market leader in the last fifteen years. After years of disappointing performance, Ralston announced the planned sale of Eveready. Bill Jockle, a strategy consultant who follows the industry closely, believes that "they never really understood what they had."[8]

Finally, the lack of a common culture and common understanding can mean that the combined efforts that were supposed to result from the acquisition—the synergies of common distribution channels, for example—never really come to fruition. It's not so unusual for the relationship to become a financial tug-of-war: The acquired company keeps trying to get more resources from the acquirer. This in turn puts pressure on the acquisition to contribute more to organizational profitability. This is the classic dysfunctional family—corporate style. And a diversified group of businesses in which people feel that the parent company "does not understand us" is not likely to provide a real cushion against the vicissitudes of the core marketplace.

What is the solution, then? When does an alignment make strategic sense?

Know Thy Business

Buying a company in a different business and allowing it to operate autonomously works best when there is no overlap in products, markets, or technology yet the two businesses are related enough for there to be knowledge on both sides about the other's operations. This puts the acquirer in a much better position to add value. It occurs most often when there was a relationship between the two companies before the acquisition; the most common examples are back or forward integrations, that is, buying a supplier or buying a customer.

When Geon, for example, bought an engineered film business in 1998, it did not know much directly about engineered film, but it had been selling to the company in question for fifty years. Geon's leaders therefore not only knew the people and culture of the business, they also understood a great deal about its supply chain and its manufacturing processes. Furthermore, the businesses were related enough that the same kinds of issues—environmental issues, health and safety issues, production technology issues—were crucial for both businesses.

In fact, the person who was in charge of Geon's acquisition deal team, Don Knechtges, used what he calls a "two-out-of-three rule" (the three being company, industry, market): He has to be familiar with at least two out of the three before considering an acquisition, and he prefers to know all three.[9]

Like Geon's purchase of the engineered film company, many alignments serve as platforms for growth in a related industry that has high growth potential (or that could have such potential if the structural determinants of growth can be changed). Or an established company may come up with a new product that serves a new market and decide to set it up as a separate business. The business is allowed to grow in its own environment in order to realize its full potential.

Affiliated Computer Services has a firm policy of only buying companies in businesses it really understands. "They know a lot about what you do, so I think that helps to eliminate a lot of the mis-expectations, if that's the right way to say it, where they may have sought something different than we were able to deliver," says Lynn Blodgett.[10]

There may also be linkages like complementary products, related markets, and similar processes. If the same factors, like the pace of technological change, are likely to have similar effects on the two companies or if the markets in which they operate have identifiable features in common, better management and strategic judgments are likely to be made. Coordinating marketing tactics across businesses may also be used, such as discounting complementary products when appropriate.

The promotional efforts that Viacom, the entertainment giant, launched to publicize *Rugrats*, Nickelodeon's first animated film, are a good example of a corporation aligning and synthesizing its business units to achieve synergy. Viacom, the corporate umbrella under which Nickelodeon operates, used its television venues to create a "buzz" about the kiddie movie—based on a successful Nickelodeon series—before it ever opened. A special about it was aired on Showtime, one of Viacom's cable networks, and numerous stories about it appeared on *Entertainment Tonight*. Since the Viacom group also includes the companies that were offering Rugrats books and Rugrats toys, as well as the home video company (Paramount) that was issuing it on video and the video chain (Blockbuster) that rented it, its promotional efforts for the film had wide repercussions for the company as a whole.[11]

The 1995 UPS acquisition of SonicAir, which inventories high-tech parts and delivers them with a few hours' notice to companies around the world, is another of our examples of successful acquisitions. This integration illustrates several important points. To begin with, UPS had originally planned to consolidate SonicAir with its own operations. As UPS's leaders learned more about the differences between the two business models, the decision evolved in the course of the integration planning process, and they opted for an alignment instead.

SonicAir has continued to operate autonomously, while taking advantage of UPS's IT and telecommunications resources, some of UPS's purchasing agreements, and some of its corporate functions. The result has been exponential growth.

As David Abney, a longtime UPS executive who was made president and COO of SonicAir when UPS bought it, explains:

> In the past, any time UPS had bought a company we had converted it fairly quickly to UPS's way of doing things. In this case we recognized several things that made us decide to do something a little different.
>
> One is that in its own market—service parts logistics—SonicAir was the market leader, so we wanted to take advantage of their position. Two, not all of SonicAir's customers were UPS customers. They used some of the other integrators and had excellent relationships not only with SonicAir but with other companies. So we didn't want to put them in a position where they had to make a choice. Three, it is a different business; we are doing a lot of customized orders and doing maybe 20,000 a day compared to delivering 12 million packages per day at UPS.
>
> So we knew that different things worked in different situations, and SonicAir had its own culture and a very loyal workforce. We just didn't feel that converting to the UPS way of doing things was going to add a lot of value.[12]

In other words, UPS executives thought about the structure of the acquisition strategically and asked themselves what kind of integration would best help them to achieve their goal for the acquisition.

Other key questions that need to be answered by a management team undertaking an alignment include: Is the relationship between the two companies clear? Does it encourage efficiencies? What will the lines of reporting be? How will financial reporting be integrated? To what extent?

Another issue that is particularly likely to need consideration with an alignment is that of the acquired company's brand: Should it be allowed to keep its former name? If the acquired company has a strong presence or a particularly stellar reputation in a market where the acquirer has less visibility, that can be a compelling reason for allowing the brand name to stand. On the other hand, if the acquirer has an equal or stronger reputation, taking on the acquirer's name or combining the two names may be preferable. Frequently, acquired companies in an alignment retain their names at least for a transition period, although this is not always the case (e.g., with Cisco's acquisitions).

People Issues
in an Alignment

On paper, an alignment looks like the most purely financial type of acquisition: Rather than attempting to meld two companies into one or engaging in any substantial exchange of managers, processes, or practices, the essential transaction simply involves an investment one company makes in the other.

Yet because it so often involves the purchase of a small, independent company by a much larger corporation, the personal emotions surrounding an alignment can be even more intense. Glenn Goldman, speaking of the numerous acquisitions he made when he was co-president of a merchant bank, says, "For the owner of a private business, who has typically poured his life as well as capital into the company, the decision to sell is always a very personal one. So the first thing you need to do is communicate up front that you recognize that."[13]

It can also be very important to win over people at all levels within a privately owned company that has just been acquired. As Goldman puts it:

Make sure you recognize and respect the contributions of second-tier managers and all employees. Deals are often structured with some part of the compensation up front and some part over time. As the management team starts getting big checks, they also start to forget why they used to get up at five and get to the office by six. Or if they're very entrepreneurial, as senior managers in small companies typically are, they might just get tired of working for someone else. Then it's the second-tier people who will be needed to do the work, so you will really need their loyalty.

In most deals he structured, Goldman set up a compensation mechanism for second-tier employees, to give them an incentive to make the acquisition work.[14]

Robert Grimes, who headed the international business development for Internet start-up Autobytel.com, has been involved in a number of acquisitions. Bob also emphasizes the importance of cultivating second-tier managers. In fact, he sees them as the key to successful alignments.

My recommendation is to make the founders of the companies consultants, rather than asking them to be involved in the day-to-day operations after the acquisition. They are just not likely to have the same commitment to the firm that they had when it was their own. And their inherently entrepreneurial nature makes it very tough for them to fit into the new framework. It's the people on the next level who are going to carry things forward.[15]

In Goldman's experience, the likelihood of a certain amount of restlessness among the entrepreneurial types in the company was so great that he structured the financial side of Conti's acquisitions to ensure that the interests of the senior managers/owners would be aligned with those of the acquirer:

When we structured a deal, we tied the post-acquisition payments not just to volume and net income but also to the performance of the loans the company originated. That way, they didn't just try to maximize volume. My advice to my people was this: Structure the deal so that you have to write—and are happy to write—the biggest check you ever made out in your life. The value you receive for writing that big ugly check is worth it.[16]

Synthesis: Best of Breed

A synthesis involves a transformation of both companies: Together, the acquirer and the acquired company become something different than either was before.

Ideally, the new organization contains recognizable elements of both companies. The image that comes to mind is of Hindu shrines in Goa, India, with crosses on top: The Jesuit missionaries, in the colony for hundreds of years, never converted many Hindus to Christianity, but gradually Christian rituals and symbols found their way into the Hinduism practiced there. The Hindus of Goa made use of those elements of Christianity that appealed to them.

Given the sort of intellectual give-and-take that is required for synergies to emerge, the free exchange of ideas between and among employees of the two companies will be particularly important in a synthesis.

For example, in 1997 when Geon bought Synergistics, a former competitor, the senior management team, comprising leaders from both organizations, focused first on learning more about each other's businesses. What were the strategic drivers within each business's market segments? Who were the key customers? What were the current capabilities of each organization? This process was essential for fostering an understanding of one another's businesses and for establishing relationships in the new organization.

The synergies that emerged from these sessions—for example, the establishment of stronger, more strategic relationships with suppliers—led to many millions of dollars in savings, contributing significantly to the success of the acquisition: Whereas there is usually a drop-off in profitability in the first year after a company has been acquired, the new business was able to achieve its revenue and profitability goals for 1998 and 1999.[17]

While consolidation and alignment both bring their own set of challenges to the integration party, a synthesis, which involves a great deal of trading of practices, systems, and staff, is often the most complex and challenging form of integration. It requires not just effective teamwork, organizational influence, and administrative skills, along with the ability to generate enthusiasm and commitment, but also an enormous amount of strategic savvy. So when is it worth going for a synthesis, and when would a simpler structural choice achieve the strategic aim just as well?

When Is a Synthesis Appropriate?

Generally, a synthesis is called for when there is overlap but not congruence between the two companies' existing businesses. Perhaps the acquired company reaches different markets with different products than the acquirer does. Or it may reach the same markets with different products. Or even different markets with the same products. If some markets are the same, and some are not, or if the acquirer excels in some areas, and the acquired company in others, a synthesis will enable the acquirer to take advantage of the strengths of the company it has just bought.

Sometimes, a synthesis allows the acquirer to merge compatible competencies in such a way that it can build a single retail franchise offering a full range of products: "one-stop shopping." When First Security Corporation, a Salt Lake City banking company, bought the full-service brokerage firm Van Kasper and Company, for example, it became possible to offer First Security's customers a much fuller spectrum of financial services—the same idea, of course, that lies behind the Citicorp-Travelers merger and the recently announced acquisition of PaineWebber by UBS, Warburg.

In other cases, the aim is to create a structure that will allow each company to continue to serve its own markets with its own differentiated products and also provide a more efficient market base; such an arrangement takes advantage of the overlap between the two companies' processes and systems. Especially when the acquired company is of significant size and includes diverse businesses, the overall integration strategy may be to synthesize the two organizations, but specific businesses may be consolidated or aligned within that overarching framework.

Even when a synthesis clearly makes sense strategically, the difficulties of executing it may cause acquirers to slip inadvertently into consolidation. With the best of intentions, it is announced that the best practices of each organization will be preserved, but when the integration effort sees the cold light of day, the acquirer's approach is almost always adopted. "What happens," suggests Bruce Brodie, veteran of several mergers in the insurance industry, "is that certain realities take over, and it becomes less than pragmatic to take the best of the best. It could be that we had a system, for example, a financial system that really was better, but it had interfaces to 600 other systems, and you're not going to change them all."[18]

This is particularly true when the two companies are very different in size. Even if the smaller company's systems or practices are superior, adopting them in the combined organization will affect many more people, and the change suddenly looks less and less important.

The trouble here, as with the "merger of equals" approach, is that expectations are established that are then not fulfilled. Trust is eroded, and the integration effort becomes more difficult to pull off successfully. Before announcing a synthesis approach, then, senior leaders need to be very clear about their commitment to this structure and the feasibility of implementing it.

Ford-Jaguar: A Successful Synthesis

A synthesis can be difficult to pull off, but there are some companies that appear to have done so successfully. As we mentioned earlier, Ford's acquisition of Jaguar in 1989 is a good example. Ford's strengths in the areas of financial control, manufacturing efficiency, and quality control made it possible to capitalize on Jaguar's own, very different strengths—a clear and established brand name, image, and unique styling.

Ford made no attempt to change Jaguar's product, except to improve its quality and reliability; instead, by combining processes and systems where appropriate, it enabled Jaguar to continue to operate in its own market niche more efficiently and to produce its highly differentiated product with greater economies of scale. The S-Type Jaguar that was introduced with great success in late 1998, for example, shared its platform and much of its hardware with the Lincoln LS sedan, although the Jaguar's suspension and drivetrains were more finely tuned.[19]

Ford's massive investment in re-equipping Jaguar's deteriorating Birmingham production facilities, where the S-Type was produced, also paid off, though it took time: Jaguar's sales worldwide had more than doubled by 1998, and predictions in the industry are that they will quadruple in the next few years.[20]

Interestingly enough, the quality processes that Ford brought to the acquisition were so thoroughly adopted and then adapted by Jaguar people that "Jaguar today has the best quality in the Ford group," according to Human Resources Director Tony Jones of Jaguar.

> We have done that by using Ford quality processes and using them very carefully, very methodically, and very consistently, adapting them to Jaguar when necessary. Ford has got lots of resources, and lots of talent—lots of smart people, and Jaguar has lunched off quite a lot of that. So, you've got a happy combination (at least I can say that today—it might have been difficult to say a few years back).[21]

As Jones implies, a synthesis is likely to take more time than other forms of integration. Soon after the Jaguar acquisition, the then Ford CFO, Allan Gilmore, was asked during an internal Q-and-A session if the investment had been a waste of money. According to Tony Jones, Gilmore replied, "Don't ask me now, ask me in twenty years." Although it may not always take twenty years to capture the value of an acquisition synthesis, a long-term view is obviously required.

Like UPS with its alignment of SonicAir or PaineWebber in its consolidation of Kidder Peabody, Ford's synthesis with Jaguar was an integration strategically planned in accordance with the following fundamental principle: The goal of an acquisition is always to add or create value.

People Issues in a Synthesis

A successful synthesis requires more work and more time than either of the other integration frameworks. This means a longer period of uncertainty for many people and a greater possibility of losing momentum in the integration.

People who are actively engaged in the synthesis effort, who are studying the two companies' systems and making recommendations for change, are likely to weather the transition period better than people who are merely "communicated to." However, careful communication

SYNTHESIS: A TIGHTROPE ACT

We have a happy combination of people who understand and have lived the Jaguar heritage along with some Ford people who have picked up the heritage pretty damn quickly.

You've got well-thought-out Ford processes that Jaguar has taken over and adapted to itself. That, combined with the financial resources of Ford has made it work. The people here have a great love of Jaguar and a love of the product, and a love of the heritage and the brand name.

The tightrope act involves using the parent company with all of its talent, resources, and abilities, while at the same time avoiding becoming simply another division of Ford, in which case we lose the brand. We've been walking this tightrope for a number of years, and I credit Ford. The Ford family and the top management of the company have been strong supporters.

SOURCE: Interview with Human Resources Director Tony Jones of Jaguar, January 2000.

planning is also especially important in a synthesis; over what may be a fairly long period of time, people need to know what decisions are being made and how they will be affected.

At GTE–Bell Atlantic (now Verizon), synthesis planning stretched out for two years in the wait for regulatory approval. Communication via the Internet helped to ease some of the stresses of prolonged uncertainty, according to GTE's Marsha Cameron: "We have a lot of different sites where employees can get information about the merger. We have gotten a lot out of that. And we have also put some self-paced development programs on the Internet to help people manage change and stress."[22]

In addition, people and teams that are hammering out the details of a synthesis may need other support, such as training in meeting facilitation, conflict resolution, problem solving, and influence skills. If they are heavily involved in the integration, they may also need to be given time to focus on these issues without the full pressures of their "regular" jobs.

KEY QUESTIONS TO BE
ANSWERED IN A SYNTHESIS

- What areas and issues require immediate attention to keep employees productive and customers secured?
- How can we share information most effectively to facilitate the synthesis?
  - How will the organization design that has been proposed promote synergy?
  - What are we doing to promote the emergence of relationships or informal structures that lead to and reward decisions that create synergy?
  - Are performance measures related to true synergy?

Making a Conscious Choice
About the Integration Strategy

In spite of the fact that acquisitions are executed to support a variety of business strategies, many acquirers tend to organize the integration of an acquired company in a similar way each time. Often, their approach is wholesale absorption. In other cases, it is simply a matter of proceeding "the way we've always done it."

When Conti Financial Services, for example, was aggressively buying home equity companies in the 1990s, the company continued to structure its acquisitions as alignments (minimal interference with the acquired company) because the initial acquisitions that had already been made had worked very well that way. However, as the number of acquisitions mounted, sticking with this approach meant that the business was failing to take advantage of potential product/market synergies and cost savings that could have been realized by similar businesses.

When those on the senior team stepped back and looked at their assumptions around the right way to integrate, they discovered that their companies were not leveraging their considerable and strong combined market presence; on occasion, their subsidiaries were even competing with each other. Although alignment had been appropriate early in the acquisition strategy, consolidation became the mandate once a certain critical mass was achieved in particular businesses and market segments.

Sometimes, senior leaders make structural choices that attempt to correct past mistakes. At Deutsche Bank, for example, the 1989 acquisition of Morgan Grenfell and Company was structured as an alignment and allowed to operate autonomously, according to a human resources executive with the German bank. After a few years, however, it became clear that synergies were not being created; at this time, the two companies were then integrated more aggressively.

Determined not to make the same mistake with the Bankers Trust acquisition, Deutsche Bank moved very quickly to consolidate the two companies, eliminating the Bankers Trust name. The executive says, "Bankers Trust was forced into the existing structure that Deutsche Bank had in place. And any product area that didn't fit, we got rid of. This was quite successful."[23]

Another successful strategy, according to some inside Bankers Trust, was that Deutsche Bank avoided, early in the integration, at least, imposing its German culture on the New York firm. Despite this reported success, however, it's tempting to wonder if a synthesis might have served Deutsche Bank better in this case and if the consolidation approach might have been an overcompensation for the U.K. integration that was less successful. At least some U.S. customers, for example, were reportedly less than comfortable about dealing with a German bank. Did the name change exacerbate that issue? It will be interesting to watch the firm's results and test this hypothesis going forward.

Building In Flexibility

It is critical for the senior team to be clear about the initial structure that will guide the integration, but flexibility of structure becomes increasingly important in building a protean organization. Scientists are finding that the most enduring biological organisms are those that have the ability to evolve their structures to survive amid unpredictable change in the world around them; the same necessity dictates the survival or nonsurvival of organizations.

Sometimes, for example, an acquirer may want to begin by aligning the acquired company, and then, as more opportunities for sharing resources or combining processes or codeveloping products become apparent, move closer to a synthesis.

The best structure, then, may be one that has built-in channels for making further structural changes. The real trick is to maintain a structure fluid enough to change its shape quickly in response to market changes, but one that is not so chaotic that the system can't function efficiently and as a unit. As with so many things in life, it's a matter of finding the right balance between two extremes—in this case, rigidity and chaos.

It's important to make the choice about the degree of integration deliberately at this point and to communicate the decision widely. The degree of integration becomes the framework for many specific integration decisions, and, indeed, for the entire integration management process. This process, which should be adapted to meet the needs of various integration situations, is outlined in the following chapter.

8

MAKING THE MARRIAGE WORK

Managing the Merger

> *There's no place where success comes before work, except in
> the dictionary.*
>
> —**Donald Kimball**, in *Webster's
> New World Dictionary of Quotations*

Despite all the work that was done before the deal is sealed, it is often
during integration planning and implementation that things begin to
fall apart rather quickly.

The major reason for this derailment is that no clear process has
been identified in the first place. Managers in units to be consolidated
are given a vague mandate to "make it work," while still being expected to fulfill all of their previous duties. People in acquired companies are told, "Carry on business as usual," without a clear sense of
what decisions will be forthcoming and when.

A general manager at a recently acquired company described his experience, which is typical of many at this stage:

> The acquirer made a big effort *not* to come out to our headquarters with
> the steamrollers and make it look like the tanks were rolling on Prague.
> That's to their credit. They were very purposeful about just sending a

few people to be friendly and say hello. Okay, Step One, we know how to say hello well.

But then what happened was either silence for two months or in a few cases some rather clumsy "Well we're going to close this data center" type stuff. We put in a few broad HR/compensation things to calm people down a bit, which buys you some time, but in essence we're still in limbo. They just really haven't been crisp about identifying the key leaders and how things are going to work.

It's like people have jumped off one trampoline, but they don't know where the next one is. In many cases, people who were empowered to make decisions for probably ten years now all of sudden are faced with talking to some bureaucrat—the decisionmaker—and they don't know what to do.[1]

To avoid leaving people in this kind of limbo, detailed integration planning is required. People need to know what the process is and when key decisions will be made. As Doug Campbell, a member of Geon's board, puts it, "The job of management toward people in acquired companies is to remove *uncertainty* as quickly as possible (even if the pain is more intense)."

This does not mean that speed of decisionmaking should take precedence over the quality of the decisions, but that decisions need to be made at a deliberate pace. Cisco's Peter Ruh believes that "speed is way overplayed. You need to move decisively, but that doesn't mean that you need to do everything in thirty days. Every deal is different for us and we go at different speeds based on what we need to get done."[2]

Even when decisions will take time to be made, at the very least, people need to know *what* is being decided, *who* is deciding it, *what* process will be used, and *when* they can expect to hear the results. It's disheartening to see how often even this minimal amount of information is not made available (most often, we suspect, because leaders don't know the answers to such questions themselves).

Although we are describing this planning work as beginning after the due diligence, it often needs to be done simultaneously, especially when the deal close date is looming. When the process works well, due diligence and planning efforts feed off each other, with information flowing back and forth. This allows for strategy to evolve as new information is uncovered.

The Integration Process

As companies become more sophisticated about integration, some are developing their own replicable integration processes. Many of the most successful are team based, involving people at all levels in resolving the issues and discovering the synergies in their areas of expertise.

Combining what we see as the best of several companies' approaches, our recommended process includes these major elements:

- The overall integration process is led by the new senior team of the organization
- An integration manager is responsible for guiding and coordinating the detailed integration process
- Integration teams are chartered to address specific areas of the integration (e.g., human resources integration, information technology integration, or integration of various business units)

The Role of Integration Leadership

In most cases, the team that will guide the integration is not the same as the deal team, which has other deals to pursue. After the deal close, there are two choices when considering who should lead the ongoing integration effort:

1. The new senior team of the combined organization
2. A separate integration steering committee that operates at a level parallel with the senior team

There are advantages and disadvantages to each approach. Having members of the new senior team guide the integration effort gives them the opportunity to shape the new organization in line with the strategies that are being formed, and it avoids much possible rework. (Once a new leader takes over, it is natural that he or she may want to change the decisions made by the integration teams.)

On the other hand, members of the new executive team usually still have a business to run, goals to achieve for their current business, and a staggering amount of work related to the integration. For this reason, some organizations choose to set up a separate integration leadership team, whose work runs parallel with that of senior leadership.

In our experience, the former approach generally works better than the latter. The work of integration is strategic work, and in the course of working through how best to integrate the two organizations, the members of the senior team also begin to learn more about one another and how to work together.

As Cisco has proven, it can be useful to have some people dedicated full-time to integration, particularly in a company with an ongoing program of acquisitions. However, it is usually a mistake to set up an integration management structure that runs outside of the real workings of the business. The work of integration is the work of the people in the businesses that are affected, with support from experts when it is helpful.

It's the same phenomenon that we saw with quality circles a few years back. Parallel organizations outside of the "real" business structure were set up to manage the ideas that were generated by the quality circles. This looked like a good idea on paper, but in fact these quality councils often broke down, and their suggestions and initiatives were often not adopted by their organizations, since they were not seen as an intrinsic part of the existing structure.

The approach we advocate, therefore, is an attempt to balance two separate, urgent, and sometimes conflicting realities. One: There is an enormous amount of work to be done in any integration, while at the same time the business of the company has to be taken care of. Two: The best people to do the work of an integration are those who are tending to that business.

In most cases, the members of the deal team or business development team are not an ongoing part of the management of the integration. The transition is made a great deal easier and smoother if at least some members of the new senior team were involved with the due diligence before the deal was closed. First, these people will have a much clearer picture of the issues to be dealt with. Second, involving them early helps to minimize feelings of resentment such as "those deal guys got us into this mess, and now we have to clean it up."

Denis Belzile, a line executive, has served as the integration manager for a number of Geon's acquisitions. In his view: "We realized after the first few acquisitions that we needed to get the business people involved from the beginning of the deal. If the business people get there too late in the game, then, after the deal is made, you have to go back to square one. After the acquisition, the integration manager starts to try and make changes, and people say, 'Hey, that's not what we discussed.'"[3]

The Role of the Integration Manager

To help the senior team drive the integration effort and maintain a focus on the integration, an integration manager can fill a very useful role. GE Capital, which is well known for its an effective approach to integrating its numerous acquisitions, assigns integration managers to manage the process—usually either "high-potential individuals or experienced hands,"[4] notably those who have served on the due diligence team for the acquisition.

These integration managers essentially serve as consultants to both GE Capital and the acquired company. They help the two organizations to understand each other's ways of doing things and to align crucial processes and functions. They are ambassadors, translators, liaisons, managers of process, but not makers of strategy. The line managers therefore don't feel supplanted, but at the same time, the expertise of the integration managers is available to ensure that things proceed smoothly.[5]

Mitchell Marks and Philip Mirvis have served as consultants on a number of integrations; they call people in this role "transition managers or coordinators." Mitchell and Marks report that in many cases these people "assume full-time responsibility—and accountability—for making the integration work." They warn that "when an executive team does not have the bench strength to free up key people for this assignment, it can be an early warning sign that the transition will not receive the resources necessary to succeed."[6]

Outside consultants can be very useful, but their role should be that of adviser, communicator, and liaison between the two organizations. Consultants should not be hired to replace a manager; instead, they should work in concert with, and under the direction of, management. There are times when it makes sense for the integration manager role to be filled by an external consultant. However, this person needs to be extremely well versed in the integration process and very familiar

---

SAMPLE: INTEGRATION MANAGER'S KEY RESPONSIBILITIES

- Review, amend, and approve the charters of the integration teams, ensuring that responsibilities and accountabilities are clear and do not overlap
- Monitor the overall integration action plan, ensuring that key milestones are met
- Provide resources to the integration teams as required, based on the strategy and new organizational structure
- Resolve issues that cannot be resolved at the team level and forward issues to senior management as required
- Identify cross-team issues that are emerging and determine how to deal with them
- Build a network of key stakeholders who will be important to the success of the changes that are planned
- Work closely with people in both organizations to coordinate integration efforts

---

with at least one of the two companies (i.e., understand the culture, the power structure, how things get done).

The Role of the Integration Teams

Even with a strong senior team and integration manager, the work of integration is far too overwhelming and far too important to leave to a few people. Cisco's Peter Ruh, who is responsible for the integration of new teams into the line business organizations, as well as critical functions such as manufacturing and information technology, puts it this way:

> If you think about it, the mergers and acquisitions process has a very small number of people involved on the front end. Because of security and confidentiality, a relatively small number of people on both sides are

actively engaged in the negotiations. Then, at the announcement, more people are involved, obviously. The public and employees become involved. Then, the connection points between the companies continue to grow as you go forward with the integration.[7]

At this point, many effective acquirers begin to form the teams that will be responsible for various aspects of the integration. The work done on these teams is crucial to the success of the integration: It is in these "blocking and tackling" meetings, where very detailed plans are worked out, that the true synergies emerge and the really sticky issues come to the fore.

As Harvey Firestone said, "Success is the sum of detail. It might perhaps be pleasing to imagine oneself beyond detail and engaged only in great things, but as I have often observed, if one attends only to great things and lets the little things pass, the great things become little; that is, the business shrinks."[8]

People's performance on the integration teams can form the basis for future staffing decisions: The kinds of skills and behaviors that are required to be effective are exactly those that will be needed to keep the protean corporation successful after the companies are merged.

The best-functioning integration teams have a clear charter; they can be used very effectively, for example, to evaluate compensation and benefit packages, compare IT systems and plan for conversions, decide on the most efficient manufacturing processes, and develop new marketing plans. Integration teams can also be assigned to address integration issues related to a particular line of business or product grouping.

Initially, each team is asked to come up with a short-term "punch list" of issues to be resolved in the first hundred days. Particularly when the plan is to synthesize the best of both businesses, this is a time when people need to engage in the free exchange of insights and information, establishing the kind of relationships that will allow new ideas and opportunities to emerge.

Making Teamwork Work

At Geon, the integration process guidelines stipulate that at the very first formal meeting, each integration team should explicitly formulate "rules of the road" for working together. A means for minimizing and resolving conflicts is agreed on, as are benchmarks for open communication, respectful interaction, and maximum contributions. In the case of persistent, irresolvable conflicts, upper-level management involvement is called for.

On the other hand, it's important to recognize that a certain amount of friction between team members can be a sign that things are starting to loosen up and the real issues are being addressed.

In the beginning, people tend to be very polite and somewhat superficial in their interactions with other team members. When the disagreements and the power struggles start to come to the surface, it can often represent a step toward real collaboration and the development of a strong group dynamic—"team-building" at its best. But it's necessary to distinguish between growing pains that will lead to strength and cohesion and the kinds of internecine warfare that will make it impossible to arrive at decisions as a group.

A common but usually soluble problem with merger teams consisting of people from both companies, at least at the very beginning, is that old allegiances and old ways of doing business are not so easy to let go of. For that reason, it may be advisable to make a conscious effort not to have teams composed of, say, a preponderance of people from a single department of one of the companies. If team members from Company A are not old workmates, or buddies, then there is less of a closed circle for the team members of Company B to penetrate. (This is typically more of a problem with team members of the acquirer, but it can work the other way, too.)

There may be some culture shock when the teams first start working together. No matter how carefully the cultural due diligence has been performed and how much of a good "fit" the two companies are, there are bound to be some differences in their styles and ways of going about things. Frank discussion of these cultural differences, once they become apparent, is preferable to simply pretending they don't exist.

At Cisco, the people responsible for the business unit integration hold weekly integration meetings and, according to Mimi Gigoux:

> They pull all these people together and just literally run through a list function by function by function and all the integration items posted for that acquisition until there is nothing left to talk about. This could go on in an organization for twelve months.
>
> Peter Ruh, the head of business integration, gets our marketing people with their marketing people and they do the new product branding.

We'll get the two management teams together to decide on development time lines, some adjustments for the acquisition, etc.

They also publish wonderful meeting minutes that are really so much more than meeting minutes. They have a web site that literally shows a red light or green light on all the different finance, manufacturing, marketing, engineering, and human resources integration areas. These lights are indicators if there are open items or if the issues are resolved.[9]

Where possible, financial projections should be made for specific integration efforts, in terms of either savings or enhancements to revenue. Such figures allow a dollar value to be put on the integration effort. It is a good idea to establish success criteria as well, both quantitative and qualitative, for each key project and program. As we have seen, Cisco, for example, judges the success of any given acquisition by its retention rate. In all cases, the criteria for judging success, too, should be directly related to the strategic goal of the acquisition.

Who Should Be on the Integration Teams?

Selection of great people to serve on the integration teams is critical to the success of the integration. Integration planning is *strategic* planning, and integration decisions have major strategic impact. This is not a job for moderately effective people who have time on their hands. This is a job for the best and the brightest, the most influential, and the most tenacious.

As we have mentioned, launching the merger process, like conducting the fieldwork during due diligence, is not likely to proceed in neat, orderly stages. The discussions do not stop when the first plans are typed up, and decisions may be reversed based on the ideas that emerge during ongoing meetings and brainstorming sessions.

Accepting the iterative nature of the integration process, though it can be frustrating, seems to be a key success factor. Decisiveness is required. So is flexibility. It's a tricky balance, and not every manager is able to achieve it. People on the integration teams should certainly have shown a previous ability to drive for results, as well as to "change horses in midstream," when required.

And it's enormously helpful to have people from both sides—acquirer and acquired—involved in the integration planning. Even in a consolidation, the support of people in the acquired company is critical to success, and having managers involved in the detailed integration planning is the best way to gain their commitment. They can also help anticipate the likely impact of proposed changes on people in the acquired company.

One caveat about attempting to get widespread involvement of people in the acquired company: If that company is much smaller than the acquirer's, people will very quickly become overwhelmed trying to meet the demands on their time that the integration brings. This is a key reason, we believe, that revenues and profitability so often fall off precipitously after an acquisition. The integration (and, prior to that, the amount of work that key people expend in actually doing the deal) is so draining that it is virtually impossible to maintain customer focus and run the day-to-day business well.

MAKING THE MERGER WORK

Our culture today is definitely not the culture that it was in 1994. But it is not the UPS culture either. If I had to describe it, I would say it is somewhere in between those two.

I think that one of the things that made the integration work was that my right-hand person here was a lifelong SonicAir employee. He is Murray Everson, my VP of operations. So even though I was president of the company, we really managed the company together and I never made any major decision without Murray being able to tell me just exactly how that would affect SonicAir, given its history and culture. Murray provided tremendous insight as to how SonicAir people would relate to my decisions.

When we did identify things that we needed to change—since for the first couple of years, anyway, I was kind of considered the "UPS" guy—Murray was the conduit to make things happen. He was the one who talked about how the chance would be good for SonicAir, especially if they were things that maybe would not be viewed as favorably at first. Communication always came from him and not from me.

SOURCE: Interview with President and COO David Abney of SonicAir, November 1999.

The Teams' Tasks:
Identifying Best Practices

Even in a consolidation or an alignment, integration teams should be encouraged to identify "best practices," or things that each side does particularly well. Obviously, this is the heart and soul of a synthesis.

Executive Director of Staffing Services Jill Kastler of Bell Atlantic says:

> We try to capitalize on best practices. There may be opportunities that technology has afforded the other company, so what we're trying to do is capitalize on opportunities where the infrastructure's already been built and the function is being performed very well. Probably a third of the time you're both already there, you're doing something very similar. A third of the time one company is significantly ahead of the other, and a third of the time you wind up building something that's brand new, because you have an opportunity to collapse the two organizations and to do something totally differently.[10]

When PaineWebber acquired Kidder Peabody, Robert McKinney, who was an executive at PaineWebber at the time, remembers, "Teams were formed consisting of people from both firms, and the systems for each function—the mutual fund function, the clearance and settlement function, the retail broker terminal function—were considered separately. In each case, the team involved chose which method or process—PaineWebber's or Kidder Peabody's—was going to be used. They then formulated a plan for consolidating the two functions."[11]

When there is to be an exchange or wholesale adoption of processes and systems, the team should specifically address the issue of how this change can be managed in order to minimize disruption of operations. If each company is essentially going to keep its own processes or systems for a given area, the issue that needs to be managed is how to make the interface between the two areas most efficient and how to ensure that the two systems are compatible and can communicate easily.

While it may seem that the more short-term issue resolution done by the integration teams should follow the senior team's formulation of strategy and organizational design work, in the real world, the two processes can be expected to go on simultaneously, ideally feeding into

A VERY FOCUSED APPROACH

We were putting in hundred-hour weeks, all of us. The consolidation was announced in mid-October, and everyone knew it had to be completed by mid-January. From October to January we stopped most of our other activities.

It was a very focused approach, to put it mildly. There were very clear goals and very clear timetables. Every morning at 7:30, and every evening at 6:00, we monitored progress. So any issues that came up we were able to bat down twice a day.

We had lists and charts that were always kept up to date, so everyone knew where things stood at any point. Everything was tracked—that was critical for success. And every Saturday, for most of the day, teams reported out, and the executive steering committee got together to make the final decisions on whether to do such-and-such the Kidder way or the PaineWebber way. But there was also a lot of informal give-and-take. It led to a lot of close working relationships between people from the two companies, which formed the basis for their working together after the merger was done.

We had four practice mergers before the real thing—by the time they did it, we had all the data transferred, all the systems working, all the kinks straightened out. We wanted merger day itself to be boring. And it was!

SOURCE: Interview with Robert McKinney, head of systems at PaineWebber at the time of the acquisition, May 1998.

and off of each other. Integration teams are providing insights and input that become important elements of the strategy; the overall direction that is set by the senior team informs and guides the work of the integration teams. It is the iterative nature of this work that makes it both difficult and exciting.

Sometimes, integration teams are charged with the task of recommending an organizational design for the new entity; in many cases, the senior team itself does this work. In the next chapter, we'll look at the process of designing the new organizational structure and staffing it with the right people in the right jobs.

9

WHO DOES WHAT TO WHOM?

Organizational Design and Staffing

Managing is the art of getting things done through and with people in formally organized groups. It is the art of creating an environment in which people can perform as individuals and yet cooperate towards the attainment of group goals. It is the art of removing blocks to such performance.

—Harold Koontz[1]

Some of the most eagerly anticipated and carefully scrutinized announcements early in the integration process involve what the new organization will look like and who will fill key roles. If you go into an acquiring company on the day of such an announcement, you'll find a buzz of discussion and speculation; sometimes, in the acquired company, there is an eerie quiet, especially if few of their leaders have been named to key positions in the new company.

Organizational design and staffing decisions are often among the first to be announced, and they send powerful messages about the way in which the integration will be handled and the kinds of people who will be valued in the new entity.

Does Organizational Structure Still Matter?

Before we delve into the organizational design and staffing process, let's take a moment to look at an interesting issue: In an era when organizational structures are more fluid and less hierarchical, does traditional organizational design still matter? In a protean organization, which is constantly shifting shape, why spend time designing an organization that may need to change soon?

Also, in many organizations, there is a general recognition that power does not always result from where you sit, but rather from what you accomplish. True power comes from the individual filling the role, not just from the role itself.

Despite the fact that the structure may need to change more frequently and that people cannot depend solely on their position for power, organizational design is still an important factor in strategic success. A structure that is aligned with a business's strategies and that encourages the kind of interaction and focus that the business needs to achieve its vision provides a powerful foundation. And as many business people have learned the hard way, a structure that works at cross-purposes with the strategy can be a maddening and counterproductive impediment.

Mapping It Out: The Design Process

Once the senior team has settled on the overall integration strategy (as outlined in Chapter 7) and the integration process (see Chapter 8), the detailed, difficult, and important work of designing the new organization can begin. This, too, is usually the role of the senior team, supported in many cases by the human resources function. In large organizations, the senior team may determine only the high-level design (the top two to four levels), while integration teams that are dedicated to staffing or integrating specific business units take over to map out lower levels.

Often, it is a cascading process, with announcements made level by level. This is the approach that was used by GTE–Bell Atlantic and by Pfizer when it integrated its acquisition of Warner-Lambert. The senior team was announced first, and its members helped to shape the design and staffing of the next level; that level was announced, and the process was repeated.

Cisco takes the unusual approach of "mapping" the entire acquired organization and making all announcements at the same time, a practice it has found very effective. Within some general guidelines, the senior team of the acquired company is charged with the task. This approach is feasible because many of Cisco's acquisitions are small ones, although the company's integration leaders insist that it could work for a larger acquisition, which would presumably have more resources available for the integration effort.

Design and staffing decisions are the foundation for so much else that these, too, need to be made as quickly as possible, always keeping in mind that the quality of the decision is the primary driver. GTE's Marsha Cameron describes how her HR integration team ran into roadblocks until the high-level organizational design and staffing decisions were made: "When we had problems, it would be a disagreement at the strategy level. Quite honestly, this was difficult to resolve until we knew who the operating heads of each business or function were. Until you have a structure in which decisions can be made by the person who would be heading up that unit, some of this low-grade fever regarding strategy was very difficult to get resolved."[2]

Like the overall structural decision at the portfolio level (i.e., the mix of businesses that comprise the corporate portfolio), the organizational design decisions at the business-unit level are driven by strategy. Different organizational designs facilitate different kinds of work and create different organizational capabilities.

Organizational Design and the Integration Strategy

The extent of the design work to be done obviously varies according to the overall integration strategy chosen. Organizational design work in an alignment, for example, is generally less extensive; all that may be required is to specify the relationship between the leaders of the acquired business and the acquiring one. Who reports to whom? Will any of the positions have dual reporting requirements (e.g., the CFO of the acquired company also reporting to the head of the acquirer's finance organization)?

In a consolidation, the work is more focused on staffing—who goes into what job—than on redesign of the organization per se, since the acquiring company's structure is likely to be used as the foundation. The work to be done is related to eliminating redundant functions, locations, and so forth. Even with people who will remain with the company, determining where they will fit in the new organization can be challenging, as many jobs and even functions are not likely to be exactly equivalent or parallel.

As you might expect, the design work for a synthesis is where it can really get tough, because you're creating something new, and many more people on both sides are likely to be affected. Designing a synthesis organization will take more time and require more discussion, debate, and horse trading. At Pfizer, for example, the acquisition of Warner-Lambert, which closed in May 2000, prompted the complete restructuring of the research and development function, now called Pfizer Global Research and Development. The goal was to build on the strengths of both companies to create the world's best pharmaceutical research-and-development organization. One of Pfizer's integration slogans captured the intent: "Not just bigger, but better."

Developing the Design Criteria

To begin the work of organizational design, it is very useful for the senior team to agree on a set of design criteria, or guiding principles. These standards describe how the new organization will operate and will ultimately be used to judge how well it is functioning. They are also used during the design process to compare options. Design criteria are derived from:

- Strategic business plans and considerations: addressing the issue of how we will win (i.e., be different than our competitors) in the marketplace, as outlined in the strategic analysis
- The kinds of work required to produce and sell the business's products or services: functional activities

- Current issues facing the organization: for example, a traditional "silo" mentality when more cross-functional cooperation is required

To begin developing the design criteria, it is useful to ask the senior leaders to describe how they believe the new organization should operate. Given the demands of the marketplace, what will it take to win, and what must the organization be able to do? Within this list, which may be extensive, what are the top priorities? These criteria then serve as the conceptual "linchpins" that help resolve the strategy–structure, chicken–egg dilemma encountered at this point in the process.

Using an oversimplified example, if a business's customers in various geographical regions require significantly different products and services and a quick response time, it would generally make most sense for the business to be organized by geography rather than by product or industry served. Think of an international baked-goods manufacturer where the products sold vary greatly by region and the delivery needs to be done very quickly. In this case, regional managers (such as VP, Canada) would "run the show," and plant managers, salespeople, and regionally focused business managers who are responsible for specific product lines would report primarily to them (see Figure 9.1).

FIGURE 9.1   Example of Geographically Driven Organizational Structure

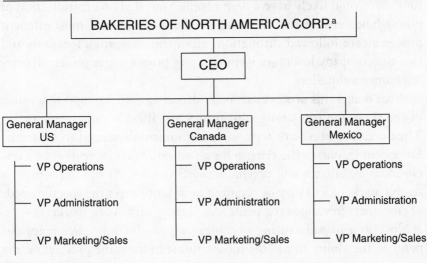

aFictional company.

FIGURE 9.2   Example of Efficient Functional Organizational Structure

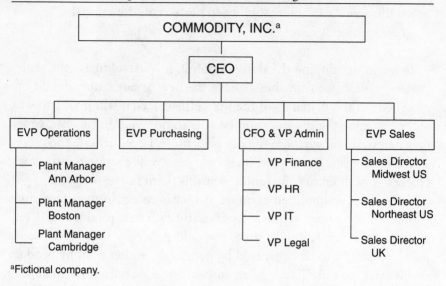

ªFictional company.

In another example (Figure 9.2), if a business's strategic success depends on its ability to be the most efficient, lowest-cost manufacturer in the industry, the head of centralized manufacturing operations might sit in a power seat, with local plant managers reporting to the person holding that position. The head of the centralized purchasing function would likely have a high profile as well. The centralization of power helps ensure that the best, most consistent, and most efficient processes are followed throughout all of the company's locations and that the company leverages its purchasing power to get preferred pricing from its suppliers.

What makes this process so much fun and so challenging is that much of the time, the top strategic priorities are at odds with one another. They create a necessary tension, and compromises need to be made. For example, one of the criteria for an automobile maker might be operational excellence and production efficiencies. At the same time, a strong market focus may be required in order to meet the specific needs of customers in various segments (e.g., luxury cars, Asian markets).

Now, in a manufacturing organization, production efficiencies depend on the ability to run the most volume of the same product on the

LINKING THE DESIGN CRITERIA AND THE ORGANIZATIONAL STRUCTURE

Leaders of a specialty manufacturing business redesigned its overall structure following a major acquisition. They established the following design criteria:

1. *Balanced decisions are made that optimize profitability.*
2. *The business is better able to deliver on its business plan, objectives, and targets (than it was prior to the reorganization).*
3. *The senior team is able to focus on strategic growth (acquisitions and integrations).*
4. *The organization is market driven: Customer needs and opportunities/threats are anticipated and addressed by market-focused decisions.*
5. *Manufacturing, technology, and distribution assets are aligned with products and markets.*
6. *Operational excellence and production efficiencies are achieved across all facilities.*
7. *New value-added products are quickly and profitably developed and commercialized in response to identified customer/market needs.*

Using these criteria as guidelines, they came up with the organizational design shown in Figure 9.3. In this structure, the director of operations is responsible for all plant locations to help ensure a consistency and efficiency of manufacturing operations (see no. 6 above). At the same time, the strategic business units (SBUs) are organized by the markets served: automobile and consumer (see no. 4 above). Within the consumer business unit, managers are also responsible for specific product lines. This focuses the SBU managers on the commercial needs of the businesses and on developing market leadership within targeted segments.

By making the director of operations and the SBU directors peers, the senior leadership of this business is sending a message that there is a need to make balanced decisions (see no. 1 above) that are both operationally sound and market focused.

FIGURE 9.3   Example of Organizational Structure Based on Criteria

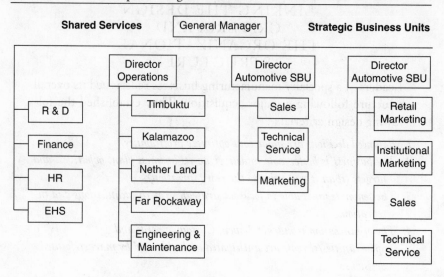

FIGURE 9.4   Example of a Matrixed Organizational Structure

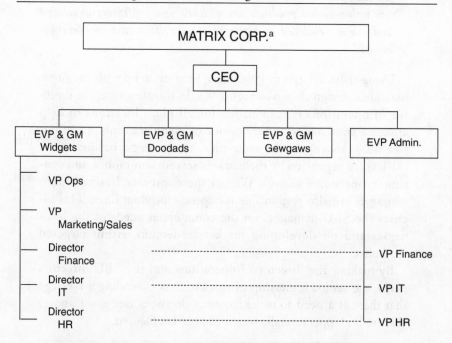

aFictional company.

same equipment. Customizing the product for the needs of different markets means having to stop a production run and make adjustments. This takes time and lowers efficiencies and run rates.

To deal with these contradictory demands, leaders often turn to a "matrixed" organizational structure, in which people typically have a "solid-line" reporting relationship with one boss and a "dotted-line" reporting relationship with someone elsewhere in the organization (see Figure 9.4). For example, in a company that is primarily organized by product line, each division might have its own VP of finance who reports to the head of the division but is also responsible to the CFO of the company.

If a matrixed structure is not managed carefully, the organization can become bogged down by the number of people whose approval is needed in order for a decision to be made. In addition, people can become confused and frustrated by the difficulty of "serving two masters," with multiple and often conflicting priorities—and therefore no priorities. Still, with all of its inherent downsides, this kind of structure is often necessary to address the complex needs of the real marketplace.

Grouping and Linking

When a team thinks through the design options that will best meet the criteria that have been established, it can be useful to consider two different kinds of organizing decisions: grouping and linking. Grouping involves deciding what tasks, jobs, responsibilities, and skills to put together or to separate. Linking involves deciding how to coordinate the efforts of different groups. At this point, the senior team is still dealing at more or less the conceptual level—what would the ideal structure look like, regardless of who will fill each position?

Grouping Options

There are three primary options for grouping, or determining what the main "boxes on the org chart" will be. Let's use a diversified financial-services firm to illustrate the point.

One of the primary grouping filters can be customers—who buys or uses the product or service? Business units, in this case, would be targeted to specific market segments, such as individuals of high net worth, small-business owners, or emerging markets in Asia. Another option is to group work in terms of the functional activity required (marketing, sales, finance, business management). The third grouping approach is to organize by the business's output—its products and services. In this case, a financial-services company would be organized into units focusing on banking, insurance, financial advice, and so on.

As you may suspect, a single company is rarely organized in only one of these three ways. Shared services such as HR, finance, and IT, for example, are often functionally driven, while at the same time, market-focused business units are focused on a specific customer slice. Still, there is often a primary grouping assumption at work, and this sends a message about what the key business drivers are and who can be expected to make the final call when differences between groups arise.

Examining the organizational groupings as they stood pre-acquisition can be particularly instructive in a merger situation. How were groupings arranged in each organization, and what does that imply about its strategic priorities and values?

Differences in philosophy related to groupings can become real roadblocks in the integration process. When a market-driven company is acquired by one where product is king, for example, there is likely to be a conflict about the best way to organize going forward. In either, case, part of the organizational design work will be to identify and resolve those differences if the integration is to move ahead.

Linking Options

Regardless of how work is grouped, few groups can operate autonomously and succeed. It's also important, therefore, to build links among groups into the organization design. Even though leaders who embraced the reengineering movement in the late 1980s and 1990s grouped work according to customer-focused business processes, there was still a need to link the business processes to one another. Customers, after all, do not really care how a business is organized—they care that their needs are anticipated and met.

Meeting these needs depends on building linkages between people in various groups. The need for such linkages varies according to the situation. Whereas people in some groups may need to work with people in other areas of the business on an hourly and daily basis, some may not really need contact at all. Such differences have at times been overlooked in the general attempt to break down silos in many companies. If the really important barriers are to be broken down, however, they need to be distinguished from others that are less mission critical.

The senior team, then, can benefit from identifying what we call "linking requirements." At this point, linking decisions concern which groups need to interact, how frequently, and what results are expected.

For example, consider an organization in which a business manager is responsible for the overall profitability and management of a product line, while the head of operations is expected to ensure that said product line is manufactured as efficiently as possible, maintaining the highest quality. Linking these two individuals and their groups is not "nice to do"; it is mandatory for the success of the strategy.

Once the linking requirements have been determined, there are a number of structural linking mechanisms that can be put in place to encourage (or force) interaction and cooperation.

The most straightforward way to link groups together is to have them report to the same manager. This is essentially a way to impel coordinated decisions at higher levels. It can be used as the basis for other linking devices, as well.

The matrixed organization mentioned earlier is another way to link groups. People's primary reporting relationships are assigned to one group, but they have secondary responsibilities in other areas of the business. A HR generalist may report first to the head of the business unit, for example, but have a dotted-line reporting responsibility to the head of the centralized HR function.

Such a matrixed structure does a nice job, typically, of linking groups on paper; in reality, it doesn't always work so smoothly. Conflicting priorities, multiple bosses with multiple expectations, and the feeling that "I'm being pulled in so many directions, I'm about to be drawn and quartered" are common, if the matrix is not managed well. If such a structure is to work, it requires:

- Agreement among the senior managers as to strategies, priorities, and resource allocations
- Great and shared clarity about individual managers' goals and performance measures
- A well-defined process for escalating issues that cannot be resolved at lower levels (that is, presenting the issue to more senior management because it can't be resolved at lower levels)
- People who are sufficiently influential, driven to resolve issues at their level whenever possible, and able to work with ambiguity

Building Informal Linkages

In addition to, or at times instead of, the above formal linking options, there are more informal ways to encourage cross-pollination and interaction between groups. Direct contact is a good one; putting people in the same physical location can make a big difference. At Ford in the mid-1990s, for example, a diverse group of 170 executives was charged with developing the strategies and organizational structure that would take the automaker into the next millennium. This Ford 2000 group was brought together in Detroit for the duration of the project, and the co-location of the people in the group was cited as a real benefit.

Communities of professionals can also be nurtured among people who share a similar education and experience base. Scientists, IT professionals, and people who sell different products to the same markets are good examples. Other informal linking approaches include migrating "straw-boss" leaders with strong ties to a particular unit to other related units of the company, building on their strong relationships.

These approaches are particularly effective when people are rewarded and recognized for results that emerge out of their informal actions. (In Ford's case, people were allowed to leave Detroit and go home.)

A final linking mechanism, which goes beyond the lines on the organizational chart, is to develop and implement common management systems across the organization. Common approaches to planning and goal setting, companywide standard operating procedures, integrated information systems, and consistent human resource policies and systems can provide a common language and avoid wasting time deciding which approach to take in a given situation.

This assumes that common approaches to these systems can be implemented in the acquired and acquiring companies in a way that builds commitment, ideally, or compliance, nominally. If new systems are imposed without the requisite buy-in, these potential linking mechanisms can develop into their own integration nightmares.

Evaluating the Options

The best grouping and linking approaches for any given integration and new organization design are those that most closely reflect the design criteria established at the outset. How appropriate is each option given the design criteria? And which has been used successfully before in each organization? Are people on both sides, for example, accustomed to operating in a matrixed environment, or would this be too monumental a change? What problems have been encountered in the past?

Perhaps more important, what are the potential upsides and downsides of particular structures and options going forward? After developing several different design scenarios, it can be useful to outline the pros and cons of each. A positive aspect of a proposed new structure, for example, might be that it is similar to the current structure, maintaining existing strengths and making the transition more palatable. A "con" might be: "The sales role is unclear with this structure—should sales people report to each regional site, or should they be centralized under one national sales manager?"

Trade-offs and compromises are inevitable. Taking careful stock of the pluses and minuses associated with each potential design can help determine the best, though never the perfect, solution. This kind of evaluation can also pinpoint the potential hot spots, or areas in which conflict can be predicted.

Designing the best new organization on paper can be intellectually challenging, and the wisest decisions are usually derived from years of experience, which are difficult to capture or replicate. Still, there is something satisfying about developing a complex, elegant organizational chart that is based on a compelling rationale. At this point, however, the design is only preliminary, and it inevitably changes when actual staffing decisions are made.

The Really Messy Stuff: Staffing the New Organization

People who have been through planning for an integration will tell you, in no uncertain terms, that staffing the new organization—filling in the boxes on the organizational chart with actual people—is one of the most difficult and critical parts of the process.

First of all, reality rears its ugly head. Even the most logical organizational design is virtually worthless if people cannot fill the "slots" effectively. Again, trade-offs are required. In some cases, a position needs to be created to house a senior manager of the acquired company who was guaranteed something substantial to do. In other cases, retention of key people may require putting them in what would otherwise be a less than optimal place.

Then there's the "quid-pro-quo" factor that feeds into many staffing decisions: If I get my guy here, I'll give you yours there. Sometimes, positions are redefined to reflect the strengths and minimize the weaknesses of particular managers. In other words, it gets "political." These are, however, real concerns that must be addressed without allowing them to dominate and subvert the process.

In some cases, the sheer scope of the task is a factor; in the merger of GTE–Bell Atlantic, for example, 41,000 people are involved. Even in smaller mergers, mapping out the configuration of the new organization and who will fit best where can be daunting.

Assessing Talent

Much of the work of placing specific people in specific jobs cannot be done effectively until the new organizational structure is built. However, this may take some time, and with retention of talent such a major issue, integration teams often cannot afford to wait to begin identifying the key people they want to keep in the two organizations.

Therefore, very early in the planning process and even during pre-close integration planning, conclusions need to be drawn about the kind of individual and group talent that exists within both organizations and who the key people are to retain.

Over and over again, successful acquirers emphasize that what they are buying when they buy a company is the brainpower, skills, knowledge, and experience of those who work there. As Cisco's John Chambers says, "You're only acquiring the employees. At the rate you're paying for them, you better not be simply acquiring the current market share of the current products, or you're in deep trouble."[3]

It has become almost a cliché that intellectual property is a company's most important asset. Yet too many acquirers don't really pay enough attention to assessing the talent of the companies they are buying or taking the necessary steps to retain those people who are responsible for its current success.

Criteria for Assessment

The existing talent within an organization, like its systems and processes, needs to be assessed in terms of both the skills and abilities of those who work there and whether the capabilities are in place to execute the strategy that has been defined for the merger. Both types of assessment are greatly facilitated if a complete cultural and human resources due diligence has been conducted prior to the deal close.

It can also be useful to get very specific about the competencies that will be required in the new organization and in specific positions. Many companies are developing competency models for specific levels or positions to ensure that they select the people with the skills, knowledge, and characteristics to perform the job effectively. Using a competency-based approach to staffing people in the new organization also increases people's perceptions of the fairness of the process.[4]

Senior-Management Talent

The preliminary negotiations for an acquisition are likely to involve the most senior managers of both companies. Even before the deal is finalized, then, leaders in the acquiring company have generally come to some conclusions about the personalities, skills, and knowledge of specific senior managers through previous contact with them, as well as being familiar with the results they have achieved.

After the deal is sealed, it is not uncommon for people to behave differently than they did prior to the closing. In the desire to do the deal, some people are careful to show only their best attributes. Post-close, problems such as clashes of ego or very different leadership styles are likely to surface, if they have not done so previously. Therefore, it's important for the leaders of the acquiring company to reexamine their conclusions related to their senior-management counterparts at several different points in the integration process.

It is also important to evaluate senior managers of both sides in terms specifically related to the challenges presented by the integration itself. Specific questions then need to be formulated to identify what leadership strengths are required for the integration to succeed and where they might be lacking or might need further development.

Those making the assessment should be encouraged to do enough fieldwork (i.e., observation, interviews with key managers, sitting in on meetings where possible) to provide answers to at least the following questions:

- What leadership behaviors and skills are currently strong in each organization? What skills might need to be further developed?
- To what extent is the leadership of each company in touch with the rest of the organization?
- In what ways are managers knowledgeable about the technical aspects of the business? Where are there gaps in this knowledge, and how does this affect the business?
- How much emphasis is there on planning and problem solving at the highest levels of each heritage organization? At middle-management levels?
- Do strategic considerations seem to be a day-to-day priority for senior managers? Middle managers?

In addition to this overall evaluation of senior leaders, people really need to be considered individually. How well do this person's skills, styles, and experience fit with this potential new job? Sometimes, in organizations with more sophisticated succession-planning and performance-management systems, information may be available about individuals' experience, strengths, weaknesses, and development plans. These data can certainly be useful in placing people, particularly when large numbers of people are involved.

It's important to remember, however, that this is only information on paper, and it's no substitute for the judgment of leaders who have worked closely with someone. For this reason, even in a consolidation, managers from the acquired company need to be involved in the staffing decisions whenever possible.

Managers and Individual Contributors

When it comes to staffing positions for managers and individual contributors, the work can actually begin prior to the deal closing. In their fieldwork within the candidate organization, members of the due diligence team and integration planning team are likely to have come into contact with or to have heard about people who are outstanding performers. By pooling their impressions of what they have seen and heard, they can begin to compile a list of exceptional managers and individual contributors. They might also want to interview some of these people directly to begin to understand what is important to them.

Post-close, in order to amass the most complete list possible of "most valuable players" in the organization, it may be helpful for interviewers to ask key senior managers questions about their star people. They might be asked, for example:

- Who exemplifies the "best and the brightest" in your company?
- Which individuals show the highest potential, in your opinion? What is it about them that makes you perceive them that way? (Here the interviewer should probe for specific examples of excellence in this person's behavior.)

There are also informal ways of identifying high-potential managers and individual contributors. As the integration process begins, certain names will be mentioned more frequently than others. If leaders are

SENIOR LEVEL STAFFING AT
BP AMOCO/ARCO

At the start of the acquisition process, I had the role of working with the head of BP Amoco's integration teams and ARCO's senior management to identify ARCO's senior-level talent for potential opportunities within BP Amoco. Basically, we took them through ARCO's Executive Resource Review process, sharing only the factual data from our executive profiles—what the person had accomplished, their job experiences, qualifications, etc. We didn't give them what would be considered more subjective information, such as our management assessment data, the psychological assessments we put our leadership through every three to five years. We didn't talk to them about strengths, weaknesses, or our views of individuals. In the pre-acquisition stage, we just told them, "This is our leadership pool, and you really need to try to attract a number of them."

It was a given that the top five executives would leave on closure of the deal. We identified talent starting at the next level, at the level below, which would be from our corporate-officer level down to what we call our bonus-eligible level. This would be considered our leadership pool and numbers about 200 within ARCO.

For the most part, it was pretty positive: We've had a lot of downsizing over the last few years, so our people are quite good. What was interesting was that BP had acquired Amoco the previous year, and I think they thought that ARCO employees would be similar to Amoco employees. They had just reorganized as a result of the Amoco acquisition and did not want to upset the new organization

(continues)

---

alert to such clues, they will make a note of those names and probe for the kind of anecdotal, informal information that could provide insight into a particular person's unique skills and qualities.

There may be an important R and D scientist, for example, who, disinclined to management work, does not appear on the organizational chart but is the source of important patents or research. Or a project coordinator may have years of experience and be the only one in a department who knows where to find important historical information.

Whether it happens before or after the close of the deal, asking managers to assess their own strengths and weaknesses, while probing for

(continued)

for the sake of introducing more (as they saw it) of the same type of employee. When they actually started meeting ARCO employees and working with them, they appeared to be very impressed and therefore made a significant effort to try and attract the ARCO people. Also, BP had had some very negative press around their dealings with Amoco employees, and they were experiencing ongoing fallout, with Amoco employees leaving the organization. So it seemed they really wanted to make amends in some way by accommodating ARCO people.

From the start, most ARCO people had no expectation whatsoever of being offered positions within BP Amoco. As far as they were concerned this was an acquisition, it was not a merger, and the thought was that there were not going to be opportunities for them. BP Amoco, however, has attempted to offer many employees an opportunity to join them. They have a considerable number of openings within the organization.

Initially they told us, basically, "We've just gone through this merger with Amoco, we don't want to disrupt an organization we have just taken a lot of time to put into place. So, we'll only be trying to fit ARCO employees in where we have real openings." But they went from that position to attempting to upgrade their organization with ARCO employees.

SOURCE: Interview with VP of Executive and Management Development Grace MacArthur of ARCO, December 1999.

---

corroborative evidence by asking what sort of feedback they receive from others, will probably give rise to some interesting answers. Ask them to describe how they see their roles as managers, or draw them out about a recent project they managed. What were the parameters of the task? How did they approach it? What was achieved? What obstacles did they face, and how did they overcome them?

Robert Silver of PaineWebber, reflecting on PaineWebber's acquisition of Kidder Peabody in 1993, comments: "From Day One, you have to ask the question, Who is it who really makes the difference around here? Who are the key people? If this individual left, what would happen? Who are the real leaders in this organization? Generally, you can tell pretty quickly just by talking to people. Upper management will tell you, 'These are the people I'd like to take with me if I were starting a firm.'"[5]

Finally, based on everything they've heard and observed, interviewers and other people responsible for staffing decisions need to identify those people whose commitment to the acquisition and the integration process will be key to the success of the effort. These might not be senior executives or even necessarily managers; instead, they might be people who are well respected in the organization above and beyond the formal roles they play. It's important to keep in mind that key personnel and senior executives are not always the same people. As Bob Grimes of Autobytel.com, says, "You can't always gauge a person's real importance from a job description."[6]

Retaining Key Talent

Once outstanding performers have been identified, it's important to determine what will keep them in the organization and satisfied in a job. How much autonomy do they require? Input into decisions? Public recognition? Rewards? A flexible schedule? Which changes would they welcome in their current jobs, and which would they see as unacceptable?

With this information in hand, plans can be made—at times case by case, person by person—to retain key people. Retention bonuses are becoming increasingly popular; increased responsibilities, more prestigious titles, better base pay, and all kinds of innovative incentives are being used in this highly competitive "war for talent" marketplace.

When moving people into new jobs, it can be very helpful to further clarify their job responsibilities and key goals for the first year in writing. Expectations are likely to be different than they were in the previous company, and people need to know what they are committing themselves to. Since the change in responsibilities rarely takes the existing performance management and appraisal system into account, there may be a need to renegotiate goals for the current year.

Another key consideration in moving people around is, in fact, moving people around. Relocation is getting to be a stickier and stickier issue for many people. One insurance company executive recalls:

We ended up asking about thirty families to move from the East Coast to the Midwest. It was fascinating to me how unexpected and how unique the personal issues were related to these family moves. Some people refused to leave their families. Others told me, "My mother is driving me crazy and I can't wait to be 2,000 miles away." Sometimes the other spouse was the key breadwinner, or the kids would have too much trouble adjusting—I heard it all.[7]

In recognition of these issues, some firms are offering spouse and family relocation support and incentives for pulling up roots. Successful relocation is one key to improving overall retention rates in many companies.

Communicating the Staffing Announcements

Whatever retention policies are put in place, the announcement of key staffing decisions creates great interest and anxiety. At this time, there is no substitute for ensuring that people have face-to-face contact with senior leaders in the organization. Bruce Brodie, now with MetLife, says it well:

In terms of the leadership role, you almost have to go person by person. It can be one-on-one, in small group meetings, in larger group meetings, every combination you can think of. People need to know that they've been seen, that they're known; they need to understand what's different, and what's the same, and that they are appreciated. One lesson I've learned is that I spend a lot more time letting people know that I appreciate them.[8]

Brodie reminds us that making the right decision is not enough—communication is another critical element in the success of the integration. Actually, it is easier to talk about communication than it is to do it well. In the next chapter, we'll look at some successful and specific communication methods and how effective acquirers and protean organizations are getting the word out—and back.

10

GETTING
THE MESSAGE OUT—
AND BACK

Communications During Mergers

*Employees are anxious about the merger and hungry for in-
formation. If the usual channels do not satisfy this hunger, the
employees will decide for themselves what to expect based on
rumors, innuendo, and stories in the press.*

—**Nathan Ainspan and David Dell,**
Employee Communications During Mergers[1]

Everyone knows that communication is key, and we've all heard the
axiom that "it's impossible to overcommunicate" with people in an
organization undergoing great change. Over and over again, communication has been identified by practitioners and commentators alike
as a key factor in the success of a merger. Yet a recent survey of HR
directors of acquiring and acquired companies cited communications
to employees as the least effectively managed aspect of the integration process.[2]

Senior leaders are not in the dark about the need to communicate
with people in both the acquired and acquiring organization. But they

face some very real barriers, and recognizing these barriers is the first step toward being able to hurdle them.

What Gets in the Way?

First, senior managers leading an integration will tell you there are only so many hours in a day. As should be abundantly clear at this point, the work of integration is tough and time-consuming, on top of what was already a daunting workload associated with running the business. If the senior team is doing the strategic planning and organizational design work described in the previous two chapters, that, of necessity, consumes a big chunk of available time in the early days of the integration. Then, there are meetings with the boards of directors, with major customers, and with investors and analysts, as well as a host of other tasks related to the day-to-day operations. Time is the resource in shortest supply in many merging organizations.

Another barrier to communication for many senior leaders is an outdated notion of what effective communication means. Too many people regard communication as mere telling, as just pushing information out, often in relatively impersonal ways such as memos, newsletters, or e-mail.

But in the most effective organizations, communication also means listening and dialogue. For some leaders, it is much more challenging and even intimidating to talk straight and engage a group of people in a dialogue than to give a speech. Many executives simply don't have the skills or experience to manage an interactive session well, and they know it.

And lack of content can be a real issue. In the early days of an integration effort, there are many questions still to be answered. It's uncomfortable to say "I don't know that yet," to admit that you don't have all the answers to questions that people are desperate about. Even though it's uncomfortable, it's also absolutely necessary.

In the face of these barriers, some senior executives retreat into their offices and delegate communications to the "communications people." Now, we've worked with some great communications-staff people in companies, and they have a lot of talent and skill at crafting messages and, in general, getting the word out. But unless that message is truly felt and owned by senior executives and is delivered personally by them, it tends to fall on deaf ears.

Good communications professionals, whether internal resources or outside consultants, *can* add a great deal of value by helping executives define and clarify the key messages that they will deliver. Simplifying complex ideas is an art, and not all executives are good at it. Communications professionals can coach executives, write drafts of speeches, prepare presentations and tool kits, and build on-line, two-way communication vehicles and content.

The communications department can also identify other "key communicators" in the organizations. These people have strong communications capabilities and credibility with a specific audience, but not necessarily because of their positions within the corporate hierarchy. These key communicators can then talk with the senior executives to learn more about key decisions and messages to be communicated; they can also coach managers and supervisors throughout the company, helping them prepare to deliver the messages as well.

Even more important is helping people understand what the message means for them personally—in this case, why a merger made sense and what changes will affect them. Author and consultant Bill Jensen writes, "No matter what the new strategy, initiative, or change program is, people have the same questions: How is this change relevant to what I do? How will I be measured, and what consequences will I face? What tools and support are available? And what's in it for me? The leader's job is to help people answer those questions."³

Crafting the Message: Employee Communications

Each merger has its own logic and rationale, and that should certainly be a critical element of the initial communication plan. Why does this make sense? What has impelled it? What would happen if we didn't do this? Why is it important?

The answers to those questions are obviously different for each deal. There are two key messages, however, that should be sent by leaders involved in any integration, and these messages need to be sent repeatedly and in a number of different ways, especially over the first 100 days.

The first message is this: "We want to get the issues out on the table." In other words, we don't just want to hear the good stuff. You will not be punished for expressing concerns, or for pointing out

problems, obstacles, and risks as the integration process gets underway. We want to deal with all those things.

Second, "You can assume good intent." This is a time when people's anxiety about their jobs and what the future may hold can lead
them to read three-act dramas into every small occurrence. A security
guard at one company that had recently been acquired was late for
work. Since part of his job was opening the plant gate, others who
showed up for work that morning found the gates locked. Immediately, there were clusters of people telling each other, "I knew this
was going to happen.... I knew they were going to shut us down....
we should never have believed them when they said it wouldn't happen." He had simply overslept.

This is a time when hidden motives and hidden agendas are assumed everywhere. How can this tide of panic be stemmed at the
source? By communicating as fully as possible what is going on, what
is intended, what the plans are—and not just talking about concern
for the employees who have been acquired but actively demonstrat-
ing it. That means two-way dialogue and openness about every aspect
of an acquisition.

Like Affiliated Computer Services (remember Mark King's philosophy? "You have got to be honest about what you are doing"), GE Capital has a policy of being straightforward with acquired companies
"about what is happening and what is planned. Even when the news is
bad, the one thing the staff of newly acquired companies appreciates
most is the truth. That includes being able to say 'we don't know'
about certain areas, or 'we have not yet decided' about others. It also
includes sharing information about when and by what process a decision was reached."[4]

Communication of
the Deal Announcement

The first significant communications challenge is likely to be the announcement of the deal or the intent to do the deal. By the time effective acquirers are ready to launch an integration process, they already
have at least the initial communication plan in place. The communications effort typically begins with the announcement of the intent to
merge (or in some cases, the closing) to employees, shareholders, the

investment community, localities, and customers. The last thing you want is for key stakeholders to learn about the deal from the newspaper or the TV.

Communications to people outside the company are generally at the forefront during announcement periods. There is often a flurry of activity related to communicating with stockholders, investment analysts, communities, and the press. Bryan Simmons, who was involved in crafting communications for the 1995 IBM acquisition of Lotus describes the early communication challenges in this way:

> On June 5, 1995, I received a phone call from CNBC asking whether I had any comment on IBM's intention to acquire Lotus. Beginning with this phone call, we were trying to gather information and decide what we should be saying, while our executives and the company itself were deciding what our next move would be. It was almost a week before we could announce that what had started off hostile had now become friendly, synergistic, and ideal. There was negotiating going on all week, so leaks were incredibly explosive. These were the beginnings of the chaos.[5]

Simmons also gives this advice about dealing with the press on an ongoing basis. "We told reporters as much as we could," he said, "and then we stopped talking. We made sure to give out phone numbers so they could reach us, even if we had no further news for them. As long as they had access to us, and got a straightforward response, they were slower to speculate and to print speculations by others."[6]

The high stakes associated with the external communication plan (how will analysts and the markets react to the merger news?) can pull the focus away from the critical internal communications to employees. Again, Cisco provides another excellent role model for internal communications at the time of the deal close. Mimi Gigoux describes how much effort goes into the announcement to employees:

> About two weeks before the announcement, I notify my team that we are highly likely to acquire "Project Code Name." I have a very fluid team of very, very senior HR people and then a team of integration specialists that really manages all the documentation and data of the integration. I assign them to a deal based on their current project workload and personalities.

Their first activity is to pull together the agenda, the content, and the materials for an "announce." We create a customized packet of information that's handed to employees the day of the announcement; it contains welcoming letters from our senior vice president of HR and from our CEO, John Chambers, that are literally written for each one of the deals. Sometimes it contains just background information on Cisco; sometimes we'll get some information on the products within the business unit or line of business that they're going to be joining. Then, most importantly, we do a comparison of employment terms, benefits, etc., at their current company and at Cisco and what the differences are. This is handed out, along with some gifts, and we invite them to take it home and review the materials with their families.

The following day we kick off employee presentations in small groups, where we encourage them to bring absolutely any question they or their family have about what all this means to them and how things will change as a result of us closing and becoming one company.

The team is also pulling together two presentations that are customized for each deal. One is this employee presentation that kicks off the morning after the announcement; the other is a management-specific presentation. The employee presentation is filled with information about the milestones of integration.

People see what activities the managers are going to be focusing on over the initial month or two, and when they, as individuals, will start seeing the paperwork and terms and closure on decisions. We review a bit of history on lessons we've learned about effective integration. We keep it to fewer than twenty people in the room.

My program managers and project leaders give the presentation, and we get it done immediately. We want to communicate to those people as soon as is physically possible. One acquisition happened immediately before the holidays. I did not want people going on a long break not knowing what was going on. So we communicated to 701 employees in twenty-four hours. I had teams all over the world going before groups of twenty hour after hour after hour for about nine hours straight.

Then, my team stays on site and we have an open-door policy. They can ask us anything they want. "My wife is going to have a baby in three months—it will be after the close. Does that mean she will have to go to another doctor?" The concerns range from simple stuff like that to very complex things. "I have lots of friends in your customer advocacy organization. I know how they're organized. They don't even have an organization like my function. How in the world is that going to be integrated into your company?" We stay on-site and answer those questions and try to sustain a high level of productivity and keep the morale up."[7]

Best Practices: Communications

As the above example suggests, personal contact is one key to effective communications. Town hall meetings, Q-and-A sessions with leaders, and one-on-one discussions with key people are personal communication vehicles. PolyOne is another organization that takes face-to-face communication seriously. Diane Davie, Vice President of Human Resources, says, "It's important to just go out and spend time with people. Our senior executives conduct extensive 'road shows' and plant tours. We go out and we show that we're open to talking, and that encourages the management of the acquired company to be open as well."[8]

If they are handled well, the key advantage to these approaches is that they encourage two-way communication in ways that newsletters, e-mail, or bulletin-board postings do not. These one-way communications can still be important supporting components of a communications plan, but they should not be the primary ways to get the message out.

CONFERENCE BOARD RESEARCH ON BEST PRACTICES IN EMPLOYEE COMMUNICATIONS DURING MERGERS

Research demonstrates that employee communications strategies are being used effectively during mergers to explain the rationale, processes, and governance changes of the merger to employees. Significant attention is being given to informal communications for changes that affect employee benefits and work life. Best practices focus on helping employees cope with emotional and cultural issues, establishing two-way communications and interaction between the acquired and acquiring company, and assuring that employees become involved positively with the merger process.

SOURCE: Nathan Ainspan and David Dell, *Employee Communications During Mergers* (New York: Conference Board, 2000).

FACE-TO-FACE COMMUNICATION

Face-to-face communication is all the rage these days because it conveys an authenticity and impact that digital communication just can't match. Even so, many still can't see the benefit of taking time away from the office to speak with groups of employees at some far-flung site. The best way to win them over is to prove that their valuable time will be put to maximum use. First, make sure that local management supports the idea—this usually means making sure that the senior executive addresses local issues as well as corporate ones.... Work with the senior executive to develop a few key messages that can be communicated convincingly. But don't overdo it: the best face-to-face meetings are when the executive acts casually and does not have a formal presentation.

SOURCE: Steve Koppel and Peter Vogt, "Face-to-Face Communication That Works for Everybody?" *Journal of Employee Communication Management*, November–December 1999, quoted in *Harvard Management Communication Newsletter*, March 2000, p. 12.

In fact, once the initial announcement has been made, some of the most innovative acquirers are turning the communication equation upside down and focusing increasingly on listening rather than telling. Almost immediately, they try to hone in on what people's concerns are, so that these issues can be addressed quickly in ongoing communication efforts. It's like taking the pulse of people on both sides so that the appropriate treatment can be applied.

Taking the Pulse

In the first thirty days, focus groups, interviews, and surveys have been used very effectively to uncover the "me" issues of greatest concern. While some of these issues are predictably and remarkably similar from merger to merger, others are very idiosyncratic, depending on the two firms.

After acquiring Bankers Trust, for example, Deutsche Bank commissioned a series of interviews to uncover people's concerns. A Deutsche Bank executive based in the U.K. describes the process and what they discovered:

With the help of some outside advisors, we interviewed a whole lot of people in both entities with regard to particular cultural concerns. What was the perception of individuals toward this acquisition? Where might people have reservations or distance themselves? This generated very useful and important information.

For instance, it highlighted the fact that regardless of the fit in the business strategy, one of the major issues was that Bankers Trust has a strong Jewish population. And for some of these people, the pure fact that they were about to be acquired by a *German* firm was a major issue.

Another major concern that was particularly salient on the Bankers Trust side was the perception that Deutsche Bank would be managed in a very bureaucratic way—that they could not make quick decisions. This was a very important piece of information. We made sure that in the early stages after the change of control, when push came to shove and certain

MANAGING PERCEPTIONS

Fortunately—or unfortunately—we had the opportunity to prove how quickly Deutsche Bank could make decisions very early on. About four weeks after the change of control, Credit Suisse First Boston tried to entice some of the industry teams on the Bankers Trust side. Entire industry teams were offered jobs. We could not afford to lose them, and so we had to immediately redo the retention exercise and give them some protection for the next several years—match the offers they had received, and so forth. This was done over the weekend, and in no time, things were sorted out. This is just one example of where information we had gathered in the cultural assessment was correlated, and our quick action helped a lot to improve the perception on the Bankers Trust side.

SOURCE: Interview with a Human Relations Executive of Deutsche Bank, February 2000.

decisions had to be made, that none of this bureaucratic stuff appeared. Actually, our real management structure had already changed a long time ago. Only less than a handful of people needs to be involved for a decision—you can turn things around in no time. But we had to be sure to demonstrate that early in the integration.[9]

He acknowledges one of the limitations of using such an approach, in which the individuals interviewed are generally promised anonymity. "You know that there is an issue, but you don't know exactly for whom. But at least these things were surfaced."[10]

These findings and many others led to a series of meetings, sessions, and workshops during which people from both sides—in various product areas, for example—came together for frank discussion. As the Deutsche Bank executive acknowledges, "Open discussion doesn't necessarily mean resolving the issue, but it does help that things are surfaced. It was a very important piece early on in the process of the acquisition—to figure these issues out and then to work out programs that respond to people's concerns."[11]

In addition to one-on-one interviews, focus groups and employee surveys can also be very useful for taking the pulse of the two organizations. Focus groups bring employees from specific subsets of the organization together to gather their input and concerns; using an outside resource to conduct these sessions can help to allay some of people's confidentiality worries.

Diane Davie from PolyOne says that focus groups "start to verify and validate the intelligence gathered on the acquired company during due diligence. They help us get a better handle on what specific plans we need to put in place for the integration."[12]

One advantage of focus groups over individual interviews is that they are more efficient—more data can be gathered from more people in less time. Talking with more people also means that more people feel someone is listening. Then, too, it is helpful to understand the perceptions of as many subgroups in the organization as possible, because those in a particular location or specific function may have very different concerns from people in other parts of the company.

Employee surveys can be designed to give a fuller picture of the "climate" (or working environment), morale (job satisfaction, level of commitment), management practices, labor issues, and so on in the two companies. These may be conducted on-line, in paper-and-pencil format, or by entering responses into a telephone keypad.

A survey of the full population or a carefully selected representative sample can:

- Involve more people than either interviews or focus groups
- Generate more quantitative "harder" data about likely integration issues
- Give even more detailed information about the concerns of specific demographic groups. Specific segments of the company can then be identified as hotspots of potential resistance or turnover. In addition, areas in which morale is high can be examined to glean best practices that can then be shared with other parts of the company.
- Set the stage for ongoing, broad communication about the merger

BEST PRACTICES: USING EMPLOYEE SURVEYS DURING MERGER INTEGRATION

- Make sure the survey is linked to the business strategy. It should be introduced and positioned in the business context. It should be clear how the results will be used to support the business in meeting its goals.
- Good communication about the survey is key to getting a good response rate (and a high response rate is key to having valid, reliable, useful results). This usually means having visible senior management sponsorship and addressing any concerns related to confidentiality.
- Communicate the results and drive ownership to the lowest possible level. Involve people in understanding the results and in creating and implementing the action plans. Senior managers can be good role models by not getting defensive or discounting negative findings. One way to set the stage for this level of involvement is to get employee's input up front in the design of the survey instrument.
- Identify key drivers of the critical outcomes measured on the survey (e.g., using regression analysis, find out what is correlated with overall satisfaction or commitment). This will help you figure out what to do based on the results to improve the critical outcomes.

- Take meaningful actions based on the results and let people know that the actions are being driven—at least in part—by the survey results. Monitor changes over time based on the actions taken.
- Make sure the instrument is as short and sweet as possible. No need for a superlong survey. You'll never be able to act on all the data anyway.
- The survey items need to be as clear, specific, and behavioral as possible. That way it will be easier to figure out what to do once you get the results back. No need for conceptual or philosophical pondering.
- A mix of quantitative and qualitative data is usually helpful. The write-in responses give more of a flavor to the ratings.
- Make sure the administration methodology works for everyone involved (e.g., electronic versus paper) and is as easy and user-friendly as possible. Clear instructions are key.
- The reports should be clear, simple, and easy to understand, even if they are based on fancy statistics.

SOURCE: Terri Lowe, Senior Sonsultant, Right Manus

Terri Lowe, a survey expert at Right Manus, describes some important survey work she did during the Chase-Chemical merger:

We surveyed Chase and Chemical employees before the merger took place, asking similar questions in both organizations.

Then, after the merger took place, the new organization instituted a quarterly survey process, with randomly selected employees. Managers and the organization's senior leaders got quarterly reports on how employees felt about what was happening with the merger and in the organization. Then, once a year, we also conducted a census of all employees, which helped us make the link between employee attitudes and business performance.

Some of the questions on the initial survey were directly related to the merger. We'd ask people to respond to statements like, "This merger will provide us with a competitive advantage," to see if they supported the merger—if they saw it as a good idea. We asked: "Does the organization have effective leadership? Does it have a sound strategy?" We also asked questions about communication, how people got information, and about rewards—whether they perceived pay as being linked to performance.

The differences in the two organizations highlighted areas of likely resistance. Chemical was viewed as traditional and hierarchical, whereas Chase was seen as much more cutting edge—it offered flextime, job sharing, and opportunities to work at home. Chase was cited as one of the hundred best companies in *Working Women*'s magazine, winning awards for innovative practices.

One of the strongest things to emerge from the survey data was how worried Chase employees were that they might lose some of those programs. As a result, we realized that a lot of communication about these specific programs was needed to allay people's concerns.[13]

GTE also used a sophisticated, ongoing survey process to track shifts in people's perceptions about its merger with Bell Atlantic on a month-by-month basis. One of its advantages, according to an HR executive, is that sponsors of the survey can pinpoint areas where things are going well—where morale is high. These areas can then be studied; what are their leaders doing that is building commitment, and how can these practices be transferred to other areas of the company?

Getting the Message
Out, and Back—and Out Again

Asking the questions and analyzing the data are only part of the equation. If no action is taken or if no one knows it has been taken, these data-collection efforts are not only a poor use of time and resources, but they can actually build resentment. People begin to feel: "They keep asking us the same questions, but they never act on the answers."

How leadership responds to the issues that are raised is a key element in the success of any two-way communications effort. Leaders' responsiveness—fast, credible, and values-oriented—to issues that are raised is in and of itself a symbolic act that will build trust and leadership visibility as well.[14]

All these approaches emphasize the fact that communication is not only about getting the message out. Sometimes getting the message *back—and then out again* is even more critical. When it is done well, this process is continuous. Over time, it focuses on and is used to promote the ongoing development of the new organization—a topic we'll address in the chapter that follows.

11

KEEPING
IT GOING

*Processes and Tools
for Developing the
New Organization*

> *If I was only allowed to give one piece of advice, it would be to
> build in flexibility in everything you do. Acquisition is a
> unique business strategy. It's a unique way to initiate your
> employment. It's a unique way to hire talent, and you can't do
> any of it always one way. Just build in flexibility.*

> **—Human Resource Director of Acquisition
> Integration Mimi Gigoux, Cisco Systems**

In the previous chapters, we have focused primarily on the short-term integration that takes place in the days and months after the close of the deal. This work is critical, but not sufficient. Successful acquirers will tell you that the true integration of two companies requires a longer-term perspective. In our experience, it generally takes between eighteen months and three years to integrate two organizations effectively—to get to the point where one plus one actually equals three.

The integration work done immediately before and after the deal is finalized sets the tone and lays the foundation for ongoing integration and developing a high performance organization that is continuously improving, discovering, and exploiting opportunity. In this chapter, you'll find processes and tools for developing the new organization at three levels: the organization level, the leadership team level, and the individual level.

At the Organizational Level

Tool: Creating and Communicating a New Vision

Ongoing work at the organizational level includes the development and communication of a new vision for the new company. After all of the trauma and turmoil often associated with an acquisition, the development of a shared picture of the future helps people let go of the past and come together in the pursuit of shared goals.

As one psychologist puts it, "Most important changes ... for good or for ill have come about through individuals combining their forces in groups, whether it be that of a lynch mob or a band of missionaries."[1] As we saw in the case of Cisco, a shared vision that inspires people and gives them a clear sense of direction can be invaluable in uniting employees in merged companies. CEO John Chambers expresses the company vision this way: "We can change the way people live and work, play and learn." A common vision can be a unifying management tool. When a vision statement is used well (too often it isn't), it can become part of the consciousness of everyone in the organization, the glue holding everything together.

In Chapter 6, we discussed how Geon's leaders focused and aligned their organization continuously and repeatedly through the revision and communication of the vision and values. At Geon, and subsequently PolyOne, the development and communication of a revised vision has been used as a very effective means of bringing the new organization together following a series of acquisitions. When a new vision was created early in 2000, for example, it reflected the aims of the new organization—acquisitions and all. Discussions were held with every employee in small groups about the meaning of the vision, and most of all, the implications of the new vision for each person's daily work.

The challenge for managers is to bring the vision down from the "60,000-foot" level and to help people translate it into what they can *do* to help the organization achieve it. This requires two-way communications with employees at all levels, delving into the details about which words were selected and why.

For example, Geon leaders described the company as a "closely aligned network of businesses." This phrase was carefully chosen (and much debated); the goal was that various parts of the business would be free to operate in the ways that best suited their market environments. The phrase also implied, on the other hand, that Geon was not a holding company. Synergies and cooperation among businesses were expected and would be measured. And the vision that was rolled out in the first few months of 2000 is changing again, as the company name is, based on the merger with M. A. Hanna, announced in May 2000.

At PolyOne, the process of developing and communicating the vision reflects the culture that they are working toward. While those on the senior team certainly made it their business to communicate the vision, managers throughout the company were charged with delivering the message and gathering the subsequent feedback from the organization.

To ensure that the message was delivered consistently (which is a challenge when there are a large number of messengers), managers were provided with training and a "Meeting in a Box." This tool kit included the suggested agenda for the vision rollout meetings and a customizable PowerPoint presentation, along with detailed speaker's notes and participant materials. It also contained advice about how to facilitate discussions with employees rather than conduct a one-way presentations, along with a feedback survey that people completed at the end of the session.

While the content of this series of meetings focused on the vision, the rollout process also sent a more subtle but equally important message: Everyone's help is needed to achieve this vision. We're in this together, and everyone's input is important. Or in the words of one of the company's guiding principles, "The total involvement and contribution from every individual is what makes us special."

Another thing that makes PolyOne special is that the vision is both specific enough to help people focus and align their work with the goals of the company, yet general enough to allow room for individual initiative and decisionmaking. A balance is required. Not everyone is comfortable with this balance—some people cry for more direction. Yet the kind of culture that PolyOne is building requires that people be able to operate under this kind of ambiguity and flexibility.

A final note about visions that are effective: In our experience, they never include words such as "earnings per share," "operating income of X," or other specific financial targets. Visions describe the purpose of the organization and what it contributes to society through its products and services. An organization that views its contributions strictly in financial terms is rarely, for most people, an inspiring place to work. Given the employment options of most of the workforce today, this kind of company is heading down the road to obsolescence.

Ideally, an organizational vision reminds people that they are contributing to something worthwhile and important, rather than just earning a living. In fact, a study carried out by researchers at Johns Hopkins polled 1,533 working people and asked them to rank various aspects of their work: "Good pay" came in fifth. A sense of accomplishment, of achieving something worthwhile, was first.[2]

Tool: Building Employee Feedback Loops

As we suggested in Chapter 10, soliciting input from employees is an important element of communications in the days following the deal announcement and close. It can also be a very powerful management tool for the ongoing integration of the two organizations and for the development of the new organization and culture.

When Continental Insurance merged with CNA, for example, a culture assessment yielded interesting results, according to Bruce Brodie, who ran the technology department at Continental at the time:

> Some pretty senior, smart people were put on the task, and they did a lot of interviewing and focus groups—not overblown, but a fair amount. They put together a point-counterpoint presentation of how each culture viewed the other. What was fascinating is that each viewed the other culture as too bureaucratic—they have too many meetings; they just can't get things done. When you've been with a company for a while, you know how to work the system, and you've long since gotten used to the fact that some things take a long time. You just accept it. But when

you interface with a company that is equal in its evolution, but different, you think it's horrible.[3]

Employee surveys can be used very effectively to help leaders understand perceptions of cultural differences between people in the two companies and the changes in those perceptions over time. Results from such surveys can also be used to develop a consensus about what kind of culture will be required to succeed in the future.

For example, in 1999, a large life insurance company that had acquired a number of related companies conducted a survey of operating practices (the way we do things around here). It was distributed to the top 700 officers in the corporation. The most frequently cited *current* practices included "following the chain of command," "respecting authority," and "minimizing risk." The top practices that would be required *three years out*, according to the executives who responded, were completely different: "innovation of new products and services," "rewarding exceptional performance," and "holding people accountable for results." Because these conclusions came from people within the new company, senior leadership had both a better understanding of current perceptions and a great tool for creating change. Rather than being imposed from above, the changes required were driven by those who had the most impact on their implementation.

A baseline survey of operating practices conducted when the deal is announced can be used to track changes in people's perception of the culture over time, as well as the progress of the integration effort.

At the Leadership Team Level

Tool: Strategic Levers for Capturing Value

Strategic levers are a tool that leadership teams can use to communicate integration and strategic priorities. They represent a blueprint or priority list of the skills that will be required to create the kind of company that will succeed in the future. Some may already be clear strengths, and others will need to be more fully developed. These are the things that senior managers and people throughout the business agree to focus on across all lines of business—the core competencies of the company going forward.

In a manufacturing company, for example, supply-chain management might be a key strategic lever. The ability to do this well across all lines of business will provide a source of competitive advantage. Skills associated with this strategic lever might include:

- Forecasting demand accurately
- Planning and coordinating each step of the production process
- Identifying the costs related to each element of the supply chain
- Linking the company logistically to its suppliers in a consistent way
- Developing and using enterprise-wide information systems that allow the business to respond to different customers and markets efficiently and effectively
- Manufacturing the highest-quality products in the lowest-cost way
- Gaining advantage with customers by using supply-chain management to help them lower costs and increase flexibility

Everyone in the company will need to operate with the understanding of these levers as a foundation for future success; particular skills and levers will obviously be most relevant to particular individuals and functions. The specific actions in support of these goals will depend on the judgment of the business unit or functional heads; however, people throughout the organization should be hearing these key themes.

This list of strategic levers will likely be revised over time, in conjunction with changes in the overall direction and strategies of the evolving organization. Global management skills, for example, may become key levers over time for an organization that is only just expanding into global arenas.

These are also the core competencies that acquired companies will be asked to adopt, recognize, and adapt. At the same time, it is critical that the acquirer avoid presenting these strategic levers in an arrogant, one-sided fashion. The transfer of key skills needs to be a two-way street, with both the acquiring and the acquired companies being open to learning and migrating best practices.

Tool: Leadership Councils

The senior team of the new organization is obviously a critical driver of the integration and continuous improvement of the organization. But the team can't do it alone. It can be very useful, therefore, to identify and organize a broader leadership group, which we call a leadership council. Depending on the structure and size of the organization, this group typically includes 75–100 leaders who are responsible for the daily implementation of business strategies and integration plans.

The leadership council is a group of top managers that meets regularly, generally once a quarter. The agenda for these meetings varies, depending on the needs of the business at that time. Typical topics include:

- Review of the overall strategic direction and plans for each segment
- Feedback from the front lines on the progress and impact of the strategies to date
- Identification and resolution of key issues affecting the implementation of the strategies
- Clarification of the role of the leadership council members as ambassadors of strategy

The last topic, clarification of the leadership council's role, is particularly important. We encourage organizations to see people in this group as "ambassadors" of strategy. Their responsibilities include communicating the strategic direction and business strategies to people in their units and delineating the implications of those strategies for the specific areas that they are responsible for. As ambassadors, they are also charged with bringing issues and input back to the full leadership council and senior team, ensuring that the strategies are constantly evolving in line with changing market conditions and customer feedback.

Because these are the top managers in the organization, it can be challenging to schedule and commit to bringing them together regularly. However, the payoffs are considerable: a shared clarity about the strategy, a broader leadership base, and goals for specific organizational units that are more directly aligned with the direction of the company. These periodic meetings also help to integrate the company

more completely because they foster stronger relationships among senior managers from both sides of the merger.

Tool: Integration
Learning Sessions

From time to time, it can also be very useful to take a step back and
evaluate the key lessons learned related to the integration process to
date. Doing this in a structured and purposeful way helps to ensure
that the organization is continuously improving its ability to integrate
new acquisitions successfully and developing a core competency in
this area.

An integration learning session can be scheduled after the initial
flurry of integration activity has subsided (usually two to three months
after the close of the deal). If the organization is involved in a series of
acquisitions, it can be particularly enlightening to ask people involved
in the process to look back over a number of deals and integrations to
compare what was more and less successful.

Before the session, interviews can be conducted asking key people to
reflect on the successes of the integration process and what they would
do differently the next time. The information and opinions gathered
in these interviews is then aggregated, and a report is created outlining
key themes. This preparation provides in-depth and thoughtful input
that can be used as the basis for further discussions and identification
of best practices during the actual session.

Such integration learning sessions, which typically last four to six
hours, also send the message that senior leadership is dedicated to
continuous improvement and that acquisition integration is an important business process that needs ongoing examination and refinement.
The conclusions and discussion points from these sessions can be doc-
umented and used to communicate to the entire organization going
forward.

At the Individual Level

In addition to the efforts at the organization-wide and leadership team
levels, there are a number of tools and processes that can be used to
ensure that individuals throughout the new company support the continuous improvement and ongoing integration of the company.

INTERVIEW QUESTIONS TO
PREPARE FOR AN INTEGRATION
LEARNING SESSION

Please describe the key lessons you have learned about identifying acquisition targets (e.g., formal or informal processes, who the decisionmakers are, what kind of information is sought, how we attempt to obtain the information, and so on).

1. What is the best way to involve the acquired company's managers and employees in the decisionmaking process before and after the deal?

2. What are the key leadership roles—in the acquiring and the acquired company—that must be played for the acquisition to be successful?

3. How have we addressed the cultural differences between the organizations (i.e., assessing, communicating, and managing these differences)? What has worked? What could we do better?

4. What do you consider to be the key challenges when it comes to integrating structures and systems?

5. As you look across the different acquisitions, what specific patterns do you see emerging in those that were most successful?

6. As you look across the different acquisitions, what specific patterns do you see emerging in those that were less successful?

7. Overall, what are the major lessons you have learned about this process?

8. What, if anything, surprised you the most or did not go as expected with the mergers?

9. What, if any, aspects of the process are you still trying to determine the best way to approach (i.e., the things that keep you up at night)?

Tool: Goal Setting and
Performance Management

Goal setting and performance-management systems are used to align individuals' goals with those of the new entity. Using a cascading process, the overall company goals are used as a framework for the development of senior managers' business goals and targets for the upcoming year. These goals, in turn, inform the goals of the people who report to those leaders, and the process is extended to include all employees.

Goal setting in today's protean organizations can be quite challenging; as conditions and business strategies change more frequently, goals need to be adaptable as well. Rather than abandoning the goal-setting process, however, many best-in-class companies are reinventing it, emphasizing both accountability and flexibility. For example, goals may be established with shorter time frames for completion, or they may be renegotiated more often.

As with a shared vision, common goals can help to drive the integration process, uniting people in the pursuit of clear results. Adapting a common goal-setting and performance-management process is a key step in the integration of two companies after an acquisition. This can also be an opportunity to use the best of both previous systems and develop a new process that clearly links business goals with individuals' results.

For example, a large pharmaceutical company used its acquisition of another firm and the subsequent restructuring of the R and D division as an opportunity to revisit the entire performance-management process. The integration brought with it an opportunity for change that might not have been present otherwise.

Tool: Skill Development and Feedback

Another common approach is to offer individuals the chance to develop the skills they will need to work best in the new organization. When the newly integrated company is designed as a matrixed structure (see Chapter 9), for example, individuals may need to develop or refine the skills required to operate effectively in this kind of organization. Conflict is inherent in such a structure, with people responsible to multiple bosses and juggling multiple priorities. It can be very useful, therefore, to provide people with opportunities to develop their conflict-management skills and to outline clear processes by which conflicts will be resolved or escalated to higher levels of management.

People in a matrixed structure also need to rely more heavily on their influence skills, as they try to get work done through others over whom they have no direct authority. Feedback and training in effective use of influence and building personal power can be very beneficial, as people learn to operate in a new, complex environment. In fact, people with strong influence skills will be valuable assets to any two organizations attempting to integrate, since direct use of authority is likely to be met with resistance from the people in the acquired organization.

Giving people 360-degree feedback[4] on their skills and current style of operating can also help them develop their skills and aid in the overall integration effort. One manager reported that a newly integrated group was having great difficulty working together, as the assumptions and operating practices of the two companies were quite different. This situation turned around dramatically, he reported, when the people in the group each gave and received 360-degree feedback on their management styles. With a better understanding of their individual styles and group profile, they began to work together much more effectively.

Each of the tools and processes outlined here can become part of the management approach and fabric of the new organization. Rather than being seen as one-time events, they become "the way we do things around here" and contribute to the development of a new, shared culture and common set of goals and strategies. And as new acquisitions are integrated, these tools can be adapted and used to smooth the integration process and encourage the continuing development of the new organization.

12

CROSS-BORDER MERGERS

Notes on International Acquisitions

> *There are a limited number of common human problems to which all peoples at all times must find some solution.*
>
> —Florence Kluckhohn,
> ***Variations in Value Orientation*, 1961**

If there can be serious culture clashes between two medium-sized manufacturers in Milwaukee, imagine the potential for cultural incompatibility between a Midwestern U.S. carmaker and one located in Frankfurt, Germany. What happens when a pharmaceutical company in Kalamazoo joins forces with a Swedish company that is actually half Italian? National differences can magnify the cultural differences inherent in any acquisition, heighten employee resistance, and make the integration even more difficult. To put it quite simply, the risk of failure is even greater than with a domestic acquisition (and the domestic track record is none too impressive, as we know).

Yet to compete in an increasingly global marketplace, more and more companies are acquiring businesses outside their own borders. Firms on every continent have increasingly been engaging in such transactions: On a single (if admittedly atypical) day, October 13,

1997, more than $120 billion in cross-border European acquisitions was announced. And in 1999, Europe's deal volume more than doubled, to $1.23 trillion. Many of the acquisitions that contributed to this figure involved cross-border transactions. A merger and acquisitions wave, even involving foreign companies, is predicted for Japan,[1] where the banking industry leads the merger activity, and Internet takeovers are fueling a big surge of acquisitions in Brazil.[2]

Europe, in particular, promises to be a hotbed of cross-border deals in the next few years. In Germany, for example, companies have traditionally been disinclined even to friendly mergers, with hostile takeovers almost unheard of. Germany's unions and political leaders have typically mounted fierce opposition to any acquisition that could have resulted in loss of jobs or foreign control. In addition, the structure of German boards of directors and restrictions on the ability to sell shares of stock without the company's permission meant that few mergers went through.

All that is changing, however, with the advent of the European Union and the success of the Vodafone–AirTouch takeover of Mannesmann. German companies now have to compete in a single European capital market, and here, as in the United States, deregulation is quickly breaking down barriers to merging.

The Internet is another major driver of globalization and cross-border acquisitions. Bob Grimes, who set up much of Autobytel.com's global network of local strategic partners around the world, predicts that "within three years, any major product—furniture, cars, phones—will be globalized and available on-line anywhere in the world. The Internet firms will have their financial ups and downs, but they are here to stay as a force in the marketplace."[3]

Executives in companies outside the United States are becoming more savvy about mergers as they grow more experienced with them. Cisco's Mimi Gigoux explains:

> Initially, international acquisitions were just plain harder, because acquisitions are so new outside the U.S. Certainly, the way Cisco does acquisitions was just alien. It was new to the management of the company we were buying, whereas in the U.S., I find some companies where the leaders have gone through one or two or three or four acquisitions. But with the volume of activities worldwide, the consolidation within our industry, they actually do have more exposure to these activities now.[4]

Many of the challenges associated with cross-border deals are similar to those encountered in other integrations—only more so. The cultures are more different, the geographical distances are more draining, the management role is more difficult, the legal and regulatory restrictions are more complex, and miscommunication is more likely.

Since the issues involved in cross-border deals are amplifications of challenges addressed throughout this book, we thought it was fitting to include a chapter that focuses on international acquisitions. This serves as both an exploration of the unique issues of such integrations and a recap of some of the general best practices that apply to any integration effort.

HOW CISCO ADAPTS ITS INTEGRATION PROCESS TO A NEW COUNTRY

I had to become an expert on labor law in all of the countries in which we acquire, and even where the U.S. acquisitions had international entities. There is a similarity among the European and Near East countries in terms of how employment law works, and this dictates a lot of how you do all the activities related to the integration.

They'll all tell you that they are absolutely unique and different in each country, which they are, but there are great similarities, too. And that's a relief, because it makes it a lot easier to become knowledgeable about all these different countries and their laws. Still, we have to customize every single template, every document for that country in that language and make sure it reflects that company's culture and the national culture.

Outside the U.S., 90 percent of the comp and benefits are regulated by their governments. Because of this, tenure matters, regardless of what industry you're in. So there is an additional amount of weight on title and tenure that you just really don't see in the U.S. anymore, except on the East Coast. There's almost as much difference between West Coast and East Coast as there is between the U.S. and Europe.

In the early days, when we were nearing an acquisition that was going to have presence in countries that I had not previously worked, I would go out on a separate trip, meet with legal counsel and draft, prepare in advance, key contributor contracts and language. I would find out exactly what labor communications were required by law, and I'd prepare the materials for those. Again, they would just be draft because you always have to customize specifically for that company, but at least I had a starting place. It can be time-consuming, and I have this commitment that I'm going to communicate to the employees individually prior to closing. If I only have a twenty-eight-day close, which is what we were averaging back then, that doesn't give me much time. So I would meet with my local Cisco office, and they would usually spend some time telling me, "People in my country react this way to acquisitions." I would listen, take copious notes. I would also study on the Internet ...

But by now I have so much experience doing this work internationally that I don't have to do a lot of prep work. I have my international exceptions list and process down so I can literally wait until the announcement and I meet with local legal counsel. Frankly I'm not afraid to say to the management team I'm working with, "I don't know anything about this. Tell me about it." I'll ask them about their country's history. It's amazing how much that reflects on their corporate culture.

SOURCE: Interview with Human Resource Director of Acquisition Integration Mimi Gigoux, Cisco Systems, December 1999.

Negotiating Cross-Border Deals: Don't Underestimate the Differences

While the merger mania outside the United States is similar to that inside its borders, there are many differences in the way negotiations are typically conducted from country to country. People who negotiate cross-border acquisitions obviously need to take into account the internal politics and government regulations of the acquired firm's country. ARCO's Grace MacArthur describes some of the differences involved in doing deals outside the United States. For example:

Companies from many countries can behave naively when they are operating in a foreign environment. In certain countries, there are just some things you have to accept if you want to conduct a successful business transaction. Foreign governments dictate many of these provisions.

You also have to behave culturally in a way that is acceptable to the people you are dealing with. Significant business opportunities in the Middle East have been lost, in my experience, through ignoring cultural differences. For example, business deals have been lost to competitors who have better relationships with key ruling families, regardless of the fact that the deals offered were financially and technically less attractive. Relationships factor strongly in closing business deals in these countries.[5]

MacArthur also brings up an interesting point about cultural differences between Britain and the United States.

One would tend to think that it would be very easy to work in either culture because English is the common tongue. But there are an immense number of subtle differences in the way both nationalities transact business, which can lead to an underlying tension which is often apparent but difficult to pinpoint. Because there is this expectation that a common language equals common behaviors, both nationalities are usually quite unprepared for what they find in doing business with each other.[6]

This warning seems to hold true for U.S.-Canadian acquisitions as well. "Most Americans would think Canadian stuff is going to be pretty much like the U.S., but it isn't," says consultant Stanley Hubbard. "Canadian English has a significantly different language pattern; one of our Canadian managers joked, 'It's the same twenty-six letters, we just arrange them differently.' And of course, Quebec is French-speaking and all the sales materials, contracts, and business correspondence should be done in Canadian French. It's complicated, and it costs money to manage."[7]

"In Asia Pacific," one integration manager noted, "country by country, there are just polar differences and the cultures are so different. Extremely, extremely different. It's just an added complexity in both the negotiation and integration processes."[8]

There are also some differences from country to country in how women in the workplace are perceived, according to some. One high-level female executive told us, "I have a little bit of an issue with 100 percent male management when I get out of the U.S. I had a couple of situations where I was in negotiating meetings, and some of the individuals wouldn't even accept my business card. I think some of them assumed that I was a secretary. Even though I was introduced, I remember getting some confused glances—'Why is she still in this room?'"[9]

During the negotiations process on a cross-border deal, executives from both sides need to realize, experts say, that the difficulties—and therefore the costs—associated with such a deal are likely to be higher than with a purely domestic merger. Stan Hubbard cautions, "If you have heady ideas about the economies of scale that you'll be able to achieve, you need to cut those by 20–25 percent when you are thinking cross-border acquisitions. You've got legal and regulatory issues; you have currency-exchange issues; you have taxation issues. It gets cumbersome and expensive."[10] Bob Grimes agrees: "Structuring these deals correctly is critical. You have to consider permits, taxes, capital movement across borders and all sorts of other legal and accounting issues. You absolutely cannot shortcut this part of the process, or it will come back to bite you."[11]

The net-out, according to people who are experienced, is not to underestimate the difficulties and differences but rather to build realistic assumptions into the negotiation process and make sure that they're reflected in the price that you are willing to pay.

Buy What You Know

Given these differences and difficulties, it may be particularly important for acquirers to have a very good understanding of the seller's industry and business. Venturing into new product or service areas while at the same time entering a new country raises the risk of failure significantly.

In 1990, SMI, an Italian holding company in the copper transformation business, acquired Kabelmetal AG, a German competitor, without significant resistance or acrimonious struggle. When asked whether national cultural differences were a major factor, an SMI executive explained:

> They might have mattered a great deal, had we, as potential Italian owners, not taken pains to be very flexible.... Our commitment to locally managed firms made a difference. Moreover, we were all in the same business, had been for years, and were committed to being so. Rather than speaking German, French or Italian, we all spoke "copper transformation" as a first business language.[12]

This matter of sharing a common business focus and language is likely to be a crucial factor in the success not only of international negotiations but also of the cross-border integration process. As with other acquisitions, the evidence suggests that global acquisitions have less chance of proving profitable when the acquired company operates in an unrelated line of business.[13]

Determine Cultural Compatibility

As we noted earlier, cultural compatibility might not simply consist of having the same rituals, management styles, organizational "myths," and cultural symbols. If we look at culture as primarily an expression of underlying organizational values, then we need to identify what those values are in the two organizations and determine their inherent compatibility.

For example, do the two organizations share a commitment to fairness and community responsibility, however those qualities might be defined in their different cultures? Do they share a strong focus on the customer and on the pursuit of excellence? Even when there are differences in national or organizational cultures—one culture tolerates risk and encourages risk taking, the other does not—an underlying similarity in values can form the basis for a successful integration.

It can be difficult to sort out which issues stem from national differences and which are due to the differences in the company cultures per se. Deutsche Bank's Kathryn Komsa, formerly head of training and development for the technology and operations functions at Bankers Trust, says: "Actually, I think the issues might be less one country versus another than different corporate cultures. And the real difficulty is that people don't know each other. The issue is developing trust. I don't think anybody can overestimate the difficulties presented by time and space in that equation."[14]

We heard similar comments from several people interviewed for this book: The differences in company culture are actually more striking than differences attributable to nationality. While in certain individual cases this may indeed be true, we suspect that it is also viewed as less politically correct to identify perceived national differences.

Yet it can be important to realize that people in both organizations are likely to be operating with certain prejudices and opinions about the other country involved. One executive in an American company acquired by a British concern noted:

> American employees' overwhelming resentment of the British is really amazing to me. Our company has had a lot to do with the U.K. over the years; many British people have senior positions in our company. Reading the Yahoo! message board, there are an overwhelming number of negative comments based on the history of the two countries. You know, things like the Boston Tea Party, or jokes that you have to have a picture of the queen on the wall and change the spell checker on your PC. Some of it is friendly rivalry, but a lot of it is becoming pretty nasty.[15]

Such national rivalry is unlikely to evaporate quickly, even with management attention. However, it is extremely important for senior leaders on both sides to be aware of the perceptions and biases in each organization so that they can begin to overcome them.

Developing
Cross-Cultural Skills

One of the most common approaches to breaking down such barriers is to move people into international arenas. In many cases, acquiring companies send their own people abroad to manage the integration process and the acquired operation. Between 1990 and 1996, the number of U.S. managers sent abroad on this type of global assignment had increased by 25 percent. It has been estimated, however, that one-third of these managers perform much less effectively outside their own country. In fact, some people claim that the growth of management consultancies in the 1990s was based on companies' need to get advice on managing global acquisitions.[16]

While the difficulty of moving managers into international assignments can be daunting, there are also some notable success stories. Asea Brown Boveri is one of them. When the Swedish electrical engineering group Asea AB acquired BBC Brown Boveri Ltd., a Swiss company, in 1987, the companies' combined worldwide operations employed 150,000 people working in 850 separate legal entities in 140 countries. The transaction was not only the largest cross-border merger in Europe up to that time, but it also created the world's largest supplier of power generation, transmission, and distribution. The company also became a leading global supplier of process au-

DEVELOPING INTERNATIONAL MANAGEMENT AT FORD

Ford has had big companies in Britain, Germany, and a lot of other countries since very early in the twentieth century. The first Henry Ford started many companies around the world, and Ford of Britain was one of those. So there is a good knowledge around the company, and there has been a lot of international exchange.

You can look along the top line at Ford in recent years and find a mix of nationalities and many people who have served overseas, often in several assignments. I don't want to contrast that with competitors, but in some of the biggest automakers, it was rare for their top people to have ever done stints globally. This led to a lack of a global perspective.

SOURCE: Interview with Human Relations Director Tony Jones of Jaguar, December 1999.

tomation systems, robotics, high-speed locomotives, and environmental and pollution-control equipment.

From the beginning, management focused intensively on developing people with the skills to work across cultures. Their first task was to identify individuals who had the potential to become global managers. Over a three-month period, Percy Barnevik, the former CEO of Asea and the head of the new organization, Asea Brown Boveri, gathered information on 500 people from both organizations, personally interviewing 100 of these.

Barnevik had deliberately decided against simply selecting global managers from among Asea's people, whom he knew well; instead, he wanted to make sure that Brown Boveri's managers were equally represented. He sought the advice of senior people in both companies and carefully studied the backgrounds and records of the people he was considering for top positions.

Barnevik was looking for "people who had demonstrated the ability to lead others with humility and respect for other cultures," people who were "extremely patient and open-minded ... [able] to understand, appreciate and work within the diversity of traditions and ways of doing things in other countries."[17]

A few years after the initial merger between Asea and Brown Boveri, the company acquired companies in Eastern Europe, the former Soviet republics, and the Far East, all of which were seen as presenting complex cultural difficulties. The global managers ABB chose to coordinate resources in these regions had to demonstrate not only sensitivity to people issues but a genuine interest in and knowledge of the countries they were going to. This was especially important since they would be interacting with local people and building local networks. They were expected to speak the language and understand the culture. Their spouses, too, were expected to learn about the countries where they were going. As Barnevik says, "You can't create a Chinese network if you don't have the interest, especially with the language, which is quite difficult to learn."[18]

Barnevik organized a three-day working seminar in Cannes, France, bringing together the 250 global managers who had been selected. He explained to them the new organizational structure, the roles they would play, and the worldwide guidelines for behavior they were expected to follow. These guidelines were encapsulated in a written document that came to be known as ABB's "Book of Values." ABB's "Book of Values" explicitly states, "We must speed up the flow of managers across organizational and geographical borderlines. At higher levels, horizontal moves should be used to create challenges and opportunities. Only in exceptional cases should transfers be stopped because that person is badly needed where he [or she] is."[19]

Barnevik also encouraged his global managers to travel to other countries and staff their organizations multinationally. "How do you make a German, for example, choose people from other nationalities to work in teams? I do it by saying, 'Take your time. Travel to the United States, travel to Scandinavia and other countries, and then look at fifteen candidates or so. Talk to them, check their references within the group, and then come back with a maximum of one German.'"[20]

ABB actively and vigorously promoted team meetings among the global managers. People from different nationalities were put on critical teams and task forces together. Of course, forming cross-cultural teams, even if the team leader has selected the other members, does not automatically mean that these people will be able to work together effectively. Companies have to be prepared for initial misunderstandings and failures of communication that can add to the cost of doing business and interfere with efficiency, at least in the short term.

Not every company is going to be willing to invest the amount of time and effort in building cross-cultural understanding that ABB did. And not every company is going to have managers in-house who can speak Mandarin or Swahili or even German. In many cases, companies keep the local managers from the acquired company or hire other people in the new country.

Respect the National Culture

Respect for the culture of the acquired company is particularly important when merging across borders. In speaking of SMI's merger with Trefimetaux, its chief French competitor, SMI's Sergio Ceccuzzi commented, "We spent much time trying to integrate the entities psychologically, while signaling to the French that we genuinely valued them."[21]

Despite the fact that they moved very quickly to consolidation, Deutsche Bank executives have also made a concerted effort, in their merger with Bankers Trust, to leave the Americans' culture alone rather than expecting them to become "Germanized." John Axtell, managing director of Deutsche Asset Management, says:

> Deutsche Bank didn't ask us to change our culture and adopt their culture. They were forming one joint multinational culture, and we were a part of that. So there haven't been a bunch of people over here to teach us German, or what kind of German beer to drink, or what kind of gestures to use. Deutsche Bank has gone out of their way to try to understand what our business is all about.[22]

The acquired company should not be made to feel that it is less important than other divisions or subsidiaries or a peripheral player in the eyes of management because it is not in the same geographical area. Obviously, this rule applies to any acquisition, but it may be particularly important to keep in mind in the case of cross-border mergers, when there is some temptation to view the company abroad as a far-off "satellite" of its parent rather than a strategically central player.

A QUICK LOOK
IN THE
CULTURAL MIRROR

Any American who honestly grapples with the German Way may eventually find an uncomfortable shoe on the other foot as German thinking sheds new light on America. Here are a few views from the other side of what Germans sardonically refer to as "Amiland":

America is an uncaring capitalistic mosh pit. Workers are cast into the street by the almighty god of profits. An uncaring government provides no social safety net. By contrast, massive layoffs in Germany are rare, as unions have become so strong in some cases that they are almost co-managers of companies.

How can America profess to be a "Christian" nation, when there is a death penalty? In Germany, as in most European nations, the death penalty is verboten.

America is still the Wild West. Anybody can buy a gun on any street corner. A figure frequently reported in the German media is that on average each Texas resident owns five guns. That statistic and extensive media coverage of violence such as the massacre in Littleton, Colorado, portray a violent society that is unimaginable to Germans, few of whom are permitted to own guns.

Americans are superficial. They are open and friendly to everyone, but they don't mean it. The civility and egalitarianism that oil routine exchanges in America are viewed as a silly waste of time and effort by Germans, who tend to be warm and outgoing to their closest friends and "reserved" with the rest of humanity.

SOURCE: Reprinted by permission of *Harvard Management Communication Letter*, October 1999. Copyright 1999 by the President and Fellows of Harvard College. All Rights Reserved.

With today's technologies, which increasingly make physical distance less of a factor, it should be possible to balance sensitivity to cultural differences with a clear sense that the acquisition is very much "on the map" as far as management is concerned.

The Good News

Despite the rather daunting work required to make a cross-border integration work, and the very real differences that need to be managed, there are always similarities as well. Mimi Gigoux believes: "People have the exact same needs, it doesn't matter what language they speak or what the local weather system is like. They ask the same questions at the employee meetings. They have the exact same concerns."[23]

Tony Jones from Jaguar agrees:

> As to how an international perspective affects an integration, I would say two opposite things. First, you have to have regard for other cultures, from the laws down to the unspoken rules. At the same time, I think an international acquisition makes you realize that people are basically the same. The basic values and drivers are not any different. In the end, people are looking to be challenged. They like to feel that if they do a good job they'll be rewarded. They like to belong to something that they think has significance.[24]

As cross-border deals mushroom in this decade, it will be interesting to see how many companies can tap into these universal needs and create entities that can overcome national and cultural differences and create value.

Remembering
What We Know

Whether across borders or within one country, making a merger work and developing a healthy, flexible organization is hard work, but, as we have seen, it can be done. To summarize a single underlying success factor among successful acquirers: *They remember what they know.*

What we mean by this is that in the urgency and rush of a merger, there is a strange tendency to throw out much of what has been learned about effective motivation and management over the last forty-plus years. If you want people to accept change with enthusiasm, you have to maximize communication and involvement. If that means that you need to take more time on the front end to get people involved with decisions that will affect them, it's worth it.

People need time to develop relationships. Teams need time to build trust. If strategy is an emergent process, it emerges out of the best ideas of people throughout the organization.

And remember what we know about the key ingredients of a successful organization. It requires:

- A sound strategy informed by everyone in the organization on an ongoing basis
- A structure that is continually improving, based on an understanding of critical customer-focused business processes
- Management practices that encourage the development of effective working relationships and that recognize that conflict is inevitable—that we need a process for resolving those conflicts

And ultimately, the commitment and effort of leaders at all levels in both companies is the underlying requirement for making a merger work after the deal is sealed.

EPILOGUE
A Closer Look at the Protean Organization

In this book, we've focused on the process of integration and how it can be managed most effectively. This process, however, does not exist in a vacuum, nor is it, in and of itself, sufficient for creating a high-performing organization.

What allows certain companies to readily absorb new ideas as well as new acquisitions, to use acquisitions strategically to respond to shifts in their markets? There are a number of other specific traits that help companies build their agility and succeed over the long term. These are the vital elements that work together to create a high-performing, protean organization (see Figure EP.1). Leaders in such or-

FIGURE EP.1   The Protean Organization

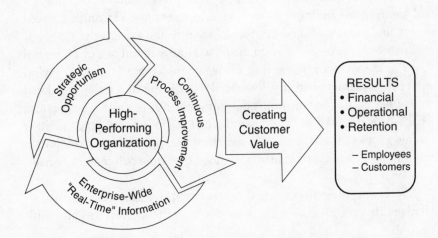

ganizations are constantly focusing on these core elements of the business in order to improve its effectiveness and keep it nimble.

Strategic
Opportunism

First, in protean companies, there is an ongoing emphasis on flexible strategic planning and the evolution of a strategy that reflects the input and needs of the marketplace. Strategic planning—neither a once-a-year budgeting process nor a binder that sits on the shelf—is continuous and dynamic.

There are repeated and widespread discussions that aim to define and refine the value proposition that the company offers to its customers: Based on what we know *today*, what will it take to win? How is this different than yesterday, and how might it be different next year? What does the most recent acquisition add to the mix? What feedback are we getting from the marketplace today, and what opportunities does it suggest? How can we seize those opportunities, and what does that imply for the strategy going forward?

Continuous
Process Improvement

Second, in a high-performing, constantly evolving organization, there is a focused, sequential targeting of specific business processes for improvement. Selected based on their strategic importance, processes such as supply-chain management, operational excellence, technological innovation, and new product development are scrutinized, taken apart, and put back together more efficiently and effectively.

Business-process improvement as we know it today can be traced back to the work of pioneering management expert Frederick Taylor. Over the twentieth century, his initial work inspired a series of related movements, including industrial engineering, operations research, work-process analysis, and reengineering. (Whatever you call it, it won't go away.) The upshot is that business-process improvement is an inherent element of managing—not a one-time program or consultant-inspired fad.

Successful integrations are also business-process improvement initiatives. To avoid becoming bogged down by the daily details and difficulties of integrating acquisitions, leaders need to ensure that the focus always remains on adding customer value. The determination of which steps, functions, or redundant processes can be eliminated during the process of integration and the unwavering focus on total quality of products and services must be oriented always toward the central goal of the acquisition—which is to provide what the customer perceives as value.

In the protean organization, the organizational structure is networked, fluid, and business-process oriented. A flexible structure both facilitates the achievement of scale economies and allows for idiosyncratic response to unique market needs. It encourages continuous improvement of business processes.

Enterprise-Wide Real-Time Information

Third, the organization's leaders are constantly revamping and improving the systems that they use to monitor the results and activities of the company. Real-time information about the key steps in the business's processes is available and easy to use. Management information and control systems become important tools for managing the business.

What has been merely talked about for the past thirty to forty years is becoming a reality today, thanks to the rapid advances in technology that are revolutionizing the way companies do business. It is now possible for everyone in the organization to have instant access to the information they require to make the decisions their jobs demand. Resources can be allocated according to what is needed where and when. Information that may be of direct value to customers can be accessed in real time, allowing people throughout the business to operate more effectively and decisively with customers.

The availability of such information makes it possible, theoretically at least, to integrate two companies more completely and smoothly than ever before. This promise, in many cases, is still far from being fulfilled consistently, as incompatible systems create their own integration issues. The more effective, more protean organizations know that resolving these issues is key and that resources need to be allocated accordingly.

Again, the key to using real-time information to maintain organizational agility is the recognition that information is not an end in itself:

It is useful only insofar as it contributes to adding value for customers. In every case, the first question to be asked is not "How efficient is this system?" or "How much will it increase the amount of available information?" but "What is it that customers want that this system will help us to provide?"

A High-Performing Organization

Finally, there is ongoing, strategically critical work to be done to continually build the organization and improve the way in which people are managed.

We now have a body of professional knowledge about what makes for high-performing organizations and teams; the seminal research began with the Hawthorne studies of the relationships among varying workplace arrangements and workers' productivity and attitudes.

We know that there *are* organizations that are run by good managers and leaders, and we know what makes them effective. There are businesses where teams *do* have shared goals and roles and are getting things done working across organizational lines.

In a high-performing organization, teamwork skills are absolutely essential—as they are to the process of integration itself. Just as the integration is a test of the company's systems and processes, it is also a test

FIGURE EP.2   Organization Flow

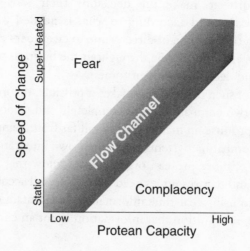

of its employees' ability to work together effectively—the same ability that will be required to respond to its changing customers and markets. Shrewd observers of the internal integration process can often predict how successfully the merged organization will be able to operate in its external environment.

Learning to Love
the White Water

These are the ongoing mindsets and practices that are required, finally, to integrate a series of acquisitions successfully. People in organizations that are shaped by these principles and priorities recognize the power of bringing people with diverse backgrounds and experiences together to create something that is positive and new. And over time, they do come to realize that change, with acquisitions being a major vehicle for change, is a fact of organizational life and, if it is managed well, an opportunity to be welcomed.

We liken this to Mihaly Csikszentmihalyi's ideas regarding how people achieve a sense of fulfillment and effectiveness. In his book *Flow: The Psychology of Optimal Experience,* Csikszentmihalyi proposes that the most rewarding human experiences come about when people balance their skills with the challenge of an activity they are engaged in. He calls the experience of balancing challenge with skill "being in the flow." We have adapted this notion to organizations (as depicted in Figure EP.2) to suggest that people in an organization experience "flow" when the speed of change is balanced with their collective capabilities to deal with change, or their protean capacity.

In conclusion, we'll quote our colleague and friend, Lance Mitchell. Lance is an executive who has led a number of integrations. After a major announcement of Geon's intent to merge with M. A. Hanna, a company twice its size, to form PolyOne, he reported:

The reaction among our employees has been very positive. People are clear that major changes will be involved. It feels like a graduation day—exciting, scary, and inevitable. Most do not see this announcement as a big surprise and tell me that it is very consistent with the strategy that has been communicated. I believe that these reactions are different from what they might have been a few years ago; people are starting to become more flexible and adaptable—to love the white water.[1]

NOTES

Preface

1. M. Scott Peck, *The Road Less Traveled* (New York: Simon and Schuster, 1978), p. 15.

2. Interview with Grace MacArthur, December 1999.

3. Interview with an executive, October 1999. (Unless noted otherwise, all interviews mentioned hereafter in the notes were conducted specifically for this book.)

Chapter 1: Acquiring the Future

1. Laura M. Holson, "There's a Steady Rush to the Corporate Altar," *New York Times*, March 4, 1998.

2. Richard J. Peterson, chief market strategist for Securities Data Corporation, quoted in "Deals, Deals, Deals," *Business Week*, January 11, 1999.

3. Nikhil Deogun, "Europe Catches Merger Fever as Global Volume Sets Record," *Wall Street Journal*, January 3, 2000.

4. "The New Alchemy," *Economist*, January 22, 2000.

5. Tony Jackson, "Survival of the Biggest," *Financial Times* (London), February 17, 1999 (citing the research of Paul Marsh of the London Business School).

6. Ibid.

7. Thomas Hobbes, *Leviathan, Parts I and II* (Indianapolis and New York: Library of Liberal Arts, Bobbs-Merrill Co., p. 86.

8. Elaine S. Silver, "In Search of Profit, Outside the Power Grid," *New York Times*, February 13, 2000.

9. Robyn Meredith, "Eaton to Retire from DaimlerChrysler," *New York Times*, January 27, 2000.

10. "Bankers Trust Officials to Get $122 Million," *New York Times*, March 23, 1999.

11. Anita Raghavan and G. Thomas Sims, "'Golden Parachutes Emerge in European Deals," *Wall Street Journal*, February 14, 2000.

12. Charles Darwin, quoted in *Economist*, November 27, 1999, p. 4.

13. For a more complete discussion of evolutionary strategy, see Stephen J. Wall and Shannon Rye Wall, *The New Strategists: Creating Leaders at All Levels* (New York: Free Press, 1995).

14. Interview with Phil Garner, May 1999.

15. Stephen Labaton, "AT&T's Acquisition of MediaOne Wins Approval by F.C.C.," *New York Times*, June 6, 2000.

16. Karl Taro Greenfield, "Do You Know Cisco?" *Time*, January 17, 2000.

17. Lawrence M. Fisher, "Cisco's Revenue and Profit Soar, As Do Its Shares After Hours," *New York Times*, February 9, 2000.

18. John A. Byrne, "The Corporation of the Future," *Business Week*, August 31, 1998.

19. Glenn Drexhage, "How Cisco Bought Its Way to the Top," *Corporate Finance* (London) 163, June 1998, pp. 21–25.

20. Ibid.

21. Laura M. Holson, "Whiz Kid: Young Deal-Maker Is the Force Behind a Company's Growth," *New York Times*, February 18, 1999.

22. Louise Kehoe, "Survey of Information Technology: U.S. Drives Progress in the Internet Age," *Financial Times* (London), March 3, 1999.

23. F. M. Scherer and David Ravenscraft, cited in Peter Passell, "Do Mergers Really Yield Big Benefits?" *New York Times*, May 14, 1998.

24. Mercer Management Consulting study, cited by Stephen Barr, "The Morning After: How to Prevent Acquisition Hangover," *CFO* 13 (7), July 1997, p. 27.

25. Simon Caulkin, "Size Doesn't Matter," *Journal of Commerce*, March 9, 1998.

26. Ibid.

27. Paige Morse, "Railroad Shareholders Sue, Delays Continue," *Chemical and Engineering News*, December 1, 1997.

28. Anthony DePalma, "U.S. Regulators Impose Fifteen-Month Moratorium on All Rail Mergers," *New York Times*, March 18, 2000.

29. Julia Flynn, Wendy Zellner, Larry Light, and Joseph Weber, "Then Came Branson," *Business Week* (international edition), October 26, 1998.

30. Ibid.

31. Interview with Dennis Lovett, March 2000.

32. Leo Tolstoy, *Anna Karenina*, trans. Rosemary Edmunds (London: Penguin, 1954; reprint 1997), p. 13.

33. Interview with Mark King, August 1999.

Chapter 2: Warning Signs

1. George Orwell, *Animal Farm* (Harmondsworth and Middlesex, Eng.: Penguin, 1951; reprint 1975), p. 114.

2. Jennifer Pellet, "Are Two CEOs One Too Many?" *Chief Executive*, January–February 1999, p. 40.

3. Thomas T. Stallkamp, interviewed by Drew Winter and Frank Washington, "We're All Here," *Ward's Auto World* 35 (5), May 1999, p. 49.

4. Keith Bradsher, "Management by Two Cultures May Be a Growing Source of Strain for DaimlerChrysler," *New York Times*, March 23, 1999.

5. Frank S. Washington, "DaimlerChrysler: Some Key People Depart; Is Daimler Running the Show?" *Ward's Auto World*, vol. 35, No. 5, May 1999, p. 49.

6. Mark Calvey, "No Matter What You Think of Hugh McColl, Jr., the Carolina Banker Rocked the Bay in 1998," *San Francisco Business Times*, December 25, 1998.

7. *Economist*, January 9, 1999.

8. Sue Cartwright and Cary L. Cooper, *Managing Mergers, Acquisitions, and Strategic Alliances: Integrating People and Cultures* (Oxford: Butterworth-Heinemann, 1996), p. 35.

9. Interview with an employee, July, 1999.

10. Interview with Glenn Goldman, June 1998.

11. Emerson, *The Conduct of Life [1860], Worship*, quoted in *Bartlett's Familiar Quotations*.

12. Interview with an employee, June 1999.

13. Stephen Barr, "The Morning After: How to Prevent Acquisition Hangover," *CFO* 13 (7), July 1997, pp. 32–34.

14. "Fatal Attraction," *Economist*, March 23, 1996.

15. Stephen J. Wall and Shannon Rye Wall, *The New Strategists: Creating Leaders at All Levels* (New York: Free Press, 1995).

16. "Fatal Attraction," *Economist*, March 23, 1996.

17. "New Sense of Direction for Rejuvenated NCR," *South China Morning Post*, November 4, 1997.

18. Interview with an employee, June 1999.

19. John A. Byrne, "The Corporation of the Future," *Business Week*, August 31, 1998.

20. Andy Reinhardt, "Mr. Internet," *Business Week*, September 13, 1999.

Chapter 3: Steering Clear of Disaster

1. Quoted in *Webster's New World Dictionary of Quotations*.

2. Interview with Lance Mitchell, February 1999.

3. Interview with Wendy R. Weidenbaum, August 1999.

4. Interview with Mark King, August 1999.

5. Interview with Robert McKinney, May 1998.

6. Interview with Don Decker, May 1998.

7. Interview with Bill Hoenes, May 1998.

8. Interview with Robert Grimes, June 1998.

9. Interview with David Abney, November 1999. Note: SonicAir changed its name to UPS Service Parts Logistics, a UPS Logistics Group Company, in September, 2000.

10. Interview with hotel chain executive, March 1999.

Chapter 4: The Mating Dance

1. Quoted in Simon Caulkin, "Size Doesn't Matter," *Journal of Commerce*, March 9, 1998.

2. "AOL Time Warner: The Net Gets Real," *Economist*, January 15, 2000.

3. Interview with Bruce Brodie, January 2000.

4. Interview with Lev Volfstun, January 2000.

5. Ibid.

6. Bill Saporito, "The Inside Story of Time Warner," *Fortune*, November 20, 1989.

7. Jenny Anderson, "Can Pfizer Keep It Up?" *Institutional Investor* 34 (1), January 2000, p. 91.

8. Interview with Glenn Goldman, June 1998.

9. This definition was adapted from the one developed by Affiliated Computer Services.

10. Interview with Mark King, August 1999.

11. Interview with Don Knechtges, November 1999.

12. Ibid.

13. Interview with Glenn Goldman, June 1998.

14. Interview with Mark King, August 1999.

15. Interview with Dennis Cocco, June 1998.

16. Quoted in Burrough, *Vendetta: American Express and the Smearing of Edmond Safra* (New York, HarperCollins, 1992), p vi.

Chapter 5: "What Have I Gotten Myself Into?"

1. Quoted in Stephen Barr, "The Morning After: How to Prevent Acquisition Hangover," *CFO* 13 (7), July 1997.

2. Interview with Bruce Brodie, January 2000.

3. Interview with Mark King, August 1999.

4. Ibid.

5. Interview with an executive, November 1999.

6. Martin (1985) and Smircich (1985), quoted in Sue Cartwright and Cary L. Cooper, *Managing Mergers, Acquisitions, and Strategic Alliances: Integrating People and Cultures*, 2d ed. (Oxford, Eng.: Butterworth Heinemann, 1996).

7. Interview with Mimi Gigoux, December 1999.

8. Ibid.

9. Quoted in *USA Today* ("Money" section), December 7, 1998.

10. Interview with Bob Silver, June 1998.

11. *Wall Street Journal*, May 26, 1998.

12. Deborah Orr, "Safe Haven," *Forbes*, May 17, 1999.

13. Doug Bartholomew, "Getting Off-Track?" *Industry Week*, October 5, 1998.

14. Scott Leibs, "Putting IT Together," *Industry Week*, October 5, 1998.

15. Ibid.

16. Quoted in Peter Fabris, "A New Balance," *CIO*, September 1, 1997.

17. Ibid.

Introduction to Part 2

1. *Financial Times* (London), May 26, 1997.

2. Simon Caulkin, "Size Doesn't Matter," *Journal of Commerce*, March 9, 1998.

3. *Financial Times* (London), May 26, 1997.

4. Stephen Barr, "The Morning After: How to Prevent Acquisition Hangover," *CFO* 13 (7), July 1997.

5. Interview with Peter Ruh, April 2000.

Chapter 6: Creating the Future Together

1. Interview with Marsha Cameron, December 1999.

2. Joan R. Kofodimos and Stephen J. Wall, "Beyond Matching Leaders and Strategies," in *International Business Strategy Resource Book* (London: Strategic Directions Publishers, n.d.).

3. "Dawn of a New Strategic Era," *RDI's Energy Insight*, Resource Data International, June 28, 1999.

4. See Stephen J. Wall and Shannon Rye Wall, *The New Strategists: Creating Leaders at All Levels* (New York: Free Press, 1995).

5. "Managing by Values," *Business Week*, August 1, 1994.

6. Interview with a manager, August 1999.

7. Interview with Bruce Brodie, January 2000.

Chapter 7: Form Follows Function

1. "The Pilloried Professor," *Economist*, May 6, 2000.

2. Ibid.

3. Amy Kover, "Big Banks Debunked," *Fortune*, February 21, 2000.

4. Interview with a senior manager February 2000.

5. Quoted in *Lessons Learned from Mergers and Acquisitions: Best Practices in Workforce Integration* (Philadelphia: Right Management Consultants, 1999).

6. Interview with Johanne Paquet Belzile, February 2000.

7. Interview with Lynn Blodgett, December 1999.

8. Interview with Bill Jockle, January 2000.

9. Interview with Don Knechtges, November 1999.

10. Interview with Lynn Blodgett, December 1999.

11. Henry Goldblatt, "Viacom's Itty-Bitty, Synergistic, Billion-Dollar Franchise," *Fortune*, November 23, 1998.

12. Interview with David Abney, November 1999.

13. Interview with Glenn Goldman, June 1998.

14. Ibid.

15. Interview with Robert Grimes, July 1998.

16. Interview with Glenn Goldman, June 1998.

17. "The Geon Company: Lessons from a Synthesis," *Manuscript*, a Right Manus newsletter, Fall 1999.

18. Interview with Bruce Brodie, January 2000.

19. John McCormick, "Ford's Influence on Jaguar," *Automotive Manufacturing and Production* 110 (112), December 1998, p. 26.

20. John McElroy, "Jaguar to Quadruple Sales," *Automotive Industries*, vol. 178, no. 11, November 1998, p. 27.

21. Interview with Tony Jones, January 2000.

22. Interview with Marsha Cameron, December 1999.

23. Interview with an executive, January 2000.

Chapter 8: Making the Marriage Work

1. Interview with a general manager, January 2000.

2. Interview with Peter Ruh, April 2000.

3. Interview with Denis Belzile, February 2000.

4. Ronald N. Ashkenas, Lawrence J. DeMonaco, and Suzanne C. Francis, "Making the Deal Real: How GE Capital Integrates Acquisitions," *Harvard Business Review*, January–February 1998.

5. Ibid.

6. Mitchell Lee Marks and Philip H. Mirvis, "Managing Mergers, Acquisitions, and Alliances: Creating an Effective Transition Structure," *Organizational Dynamics* 28 (3), Winter 2000, p. 38.

7. Interview with Peter Ruh, April 2000.

8. Quoted in *Employee Communication Newsletter*, 2000.

9. Interview with Mimi Gigoux, December 1999.

10. Interview with Jill Kastler, May 1999.

11. Interview with Robert McKinney, May 1998.

Chapter 9: Who Does What to Whom?

1. Quoted in sample issue of the newsletter *The Motivational Manager* (Chicago: Lawrence Regan Communications, 2000).

2. Interview with Marsha Cameron, December 1999.

3. James Daly, "The Art of the Deal," interview with John Chambers, *Business 2.0*, October 1999.

4. For more information about the development and use of competency models, see Anntoinette D. Lucia and Richard Lepsinger, *The Art and Science of Competency Models* (San Francisco: Jossey-Bass/Pfeiffer, 1999).

5. Interview with Robert Silver, May 1998.

6. Interview with Robert Grimes, July 1998.

7. Interview with an executive, January 2000.

8. Interview with Bruce Brodie, January 2000.

Chapter 10: Getting the Message Out

1. Nathan Ainspan and David Dell, *Employee Communications During Mergers* (New York: Conference Board, 2000).

2. Hewitt Associates study, 1998. Cited in Toby J. Tetenbaum, "Beating the Odds of Acquisition Failure: Seven Key Practices That Improve the Chance for Expected Integration and Synergies," *Organizational Dynamics*, vol. 28, no.2, Autumn 1999.

3. Quoted in Jill Rosenfeld, "Want to Lead Better? It's Simple," *Fast Company* 32, March 2000, p. 58.

4. Ronald K. Ashkenas, Lawrence J. DeMonaco, and Suzanne C. Francis, "Making the Deal Real: How GE Capital Integrates Acquisitions," *Harvard Business Review*, vol. 76, no.1, January–February 1998, p. 170.

5. Bryan Simmons, "Surviving a High-Tech Acquisition," *Across the Board* 35 (5), May 1998, p. 55.

6. Ibid.

7. Interview with Mimi Gigoux, December 1999.

8. Interview with Diane Davie, February 2000.

9. Interview with an executive, February 2000.

10. Ibid.

11. Ibid.

12. Interview with Diane Davie, February 2000.

13. Interview with Terri Lowe, June 1999.

14. Thanks to Carol Ann Taggart of Right Management Consultants for this insight.

Chapter 11: Keeping It Going

1. Petruska Clarkson, *Change in Organizations* (London: Whurr Publishers, 1995), p. 86.

2. Cited in Viktor E. Frankl, *Man's Search for Ultimate Meaning* (New York: Perseus Publishing, 1997).

3. Interview with Bruce Brodie, January 2000.

4. The term "360-degree feedback" refers to a process that provides feedback from a person's boss, colleagues, and direct reports.

Chapter 12: Cross-Border Mergers

1. Robert Nee, "Japan: Land of the Hostile Takeover?" *Business Week*, April 10, 2000.

2. Simon Romero, "Internet Takeovers Fuel a Big Surge of Acquisitions in Brazil," *New York Times*, April 10, 2000.

3. Interview with Robert Grimes, February 2000.

4. Interview with Mimi Gigoux, December 1999.

5. Interview with Grace MacArthur, February 2000.

6. Ibid.

7. Interview with Stanley Hubbard, February 2000.

8. Interview with an integration manager, February 2000.

9. Interview with a female executive, March 2000.

10. Interview with Stanley Hubbard, February 2000.

11. Interview with Robert Grimes, February 2000.

12. Quoted in James K. Sebenius, "Negotiating Cross-Border Acquisitions," *Sloan Management Review* 16 (2), Winter 1998, pp. 125–135.

13. Constantine Markides and Daniel Oyon, "International Acquisitions: Do They Create Value for Shareholders?" *European Management Journal*, April 1998.

14. Interview with Kathryn Komsa, September 1999.

15. Interview with an executive, June 1999.

16. Piero Morosoni, *Managing Cultural Differences* (New York: Elsevier Science, 1998).

17. Ibid.

18. Ibid.

19. Ibid., p. 249.

20. Ibid.

21. Sebenius, "Negotiating Cross-Border Acquisitions," p. 127.

22. Interview with John Axtell, December 1999.
23. Interview with Mimi Gigoux, December 1999.
24. Interview with Tony Jones, December 1999.

Epilogue

1. Interview with Lance Mitchell, May 2000.

INDEX